MznLnx

Missing Links Exam Preps

Exam Prep for

Linear Algebra and its Applications

Strang, 3rd Edition

The MznLnx Exam Prep is your link from the texbook and lecture to your exams.
The MznLnx Exam Preps are unauthorized and comprehensive reviews of your textbooks.

All material provided by MznLnx and Rico Publications (c) 2010
Textbook publishers and textbook authors do not particpate in or contribute to these reviews.

MznLnx

Rico Publications

Exam Prep for Linear Algebra and its Applications
3rd Edition
Strang

Publisher: Raymond Houge
Assistant Editor: Michael Rouger
Text and Cover Designer: Lisa Buckner
Marketing Manager: Sara Swagger
Project Manager, Editorial Production: Jerry Emerson
Art Director: Vernon Lowerui

Product Manager: Dave Mason
Editorial Assitant: Rachel Guzmanji
Pedagogy: Debra Long
Cover Image: Jim Reed/Getty Images
Text and Cover Printer: City Printing, Inc.
Compositor: Media Mix, Inc.

(c) 2010 Rico Publications
ALL RIGHTS RESERVED. No part of this work covered by the copyright may be reproduced or used in any form or by an means--graphic, electronic, or mechanical, including photocopying, recording, taping, Web distribution, information storage, and retrieval systems, or in any other manner--without the written permission of the publisher.

Printed in the United States
ISBN:

For more information about our products, contact us at:
Dave.Mason@RicoPublications.com

For permission to use material from this text or product, submit a request online to:
Dave.Mason@RicoPublications.com

Contents

CHAPTER 1
MATRICES AND GAUSSIAN ELIMINATION — 1

CHAPTER 2
VECTOR SPACES AND LINEAR EQUATIONS — 12

CHAPTER 3
ORTHOGONALITY — 18

CHAPTER 4
DETERMINANTS — 35

CHAPTER 5
EIGENVALUES AND EIGENVECTORS — 41

CHAPTER 6
POSITIVE DEFINITE MATRICES — 62

CHAPTER 7
COMPUTATIONS WITH MATRICES — 70

CHAPTER 8
LINEAR PROGRAMMING AND GAME THEORY — 79

ANSWER KEY — 91

TO THE STUDENT

COMPREHENSIVE

The *MznLnx* Exam Prep series is designed to help you pass your exams. Editors at MznLnx review your textbooks and then prepare these practice exams to help you master the textbook material. Unlike study guides, workbooks, and practice tests provided by the texbook publisher and textbook authors, *MznLnx* gives you **all** of the material in each chapter in exam form, not just samples, so you can be sure to nail your exam.

MECHANICAL

The MznLnx Exam Prep series creates exams that will help you learn the subject matter as well as test you on your understanding. Each question is designed to help you master the concept. Just working through the exams, you gain an understanding of the subject--its a simple mechanical process that produces success.

INTEGRATED STUDY GUIDE AND REVIEW

MznLnx is not just a set of exams designed to test you, its also a comprehensive review of the subject content. Each exam question is also a review of the concept, making sure that you will get the answer correct without having to go to other sources of material. You learn as you go! Its the easiest way to pass an exam.

HUMOR

Studying can be tedious and dry. MznLnx's instructional design includes moderate humor within the exam questions on occassion, to break the tedium and revitalize the brain

Chapter 1. MATRICES AND GAUSSIAN ELIMINATION

1. In linear algebra, _____ is an efficient algorithm for solving systems of linear equations, finding the rank of a matrix, and calculating the inverse of an invertible square matrix. _____ is named after German mathematician and scientist Carl Friedrich Gauss.

Elementary row operations are used to reduce a matrix to row echelon form.

   a. -module
   b. Gaussian elimination
   c. -equivalence
   d. 2-bridge knot

2. In mathematics, _____ or factoring is the decomposition of an object ' href='/wiki/Matrix_(mathematics)'>matrix) into a product of other objects, or factors, which when multiplied together give the original. For example, the number 15 factors into primes as 3 × 5, and the polynomial $x^2 - 4$ factors as (x − 2)(x + 2.) In all cases, a product of simpler objects is obtained.
   a. -module
   b. Factorization
   c. -equivalence
   d. 2-bridge knot

3. In mathematics, a _____ is a flat surface. Planes can arise as subspaces of some higher dimensional space, as with the walls of a room, or they may enjoy an independent existence in their own right, as in the setting of Euclidean geometry
   a. Similarity
   b. -module
   c. -equivalence
   d. Plane

4. In linear algebra, a _____ or column matrix is an m × 1 matrix, i.e. a matrix consisting of a single column of m elements.

$$\mathbf{x} = \begin{bmatrix} x_1 \\ x_2 \\ \vdots \\ x_m \end{bmatrix}$$

The transpose of a _____ is a row vector and vice versa.

The set of all column vectors forms a vector space which is the dual space to the set of all row vectors.

a. K-frame
b. Symplectic vector space
c. Normal basis
d. Column vector

5. _____ is the mathematical process of putting things together. The plus sign '+' means that numbers are added together. For example, in the picture on the right, there are 3 + 2 apples--meaning three apples and two other apples--which is the same as five apples, since 3 + 2 = 5.

a. ADE classification
b. AKS primality test
c. Abelian P-root group
d. Addition

6. In mathematics, _____ are a concept central to linear algebra and related fields of mathematics

Suppose that K is a field and V is a vector space over K. As usual, we call elements of V vectors and call elements of K scalars.

a. Hyperstructures
b. Linear combinations
c. Left alternative
d. Groupoid

7. If $A_1, A_2, ..., A_n$ are _____ square matrices over a field, then

$$(A_1 A_2 \cdots A_n)^{-1} = A_n^{-1} A_{n-1}^{-1} \cdots A_1^{-1}.$$

It becomes evident why this is the case if one attempts to find an inverse for the product of the A_is from first principles, that is, that we wish to determine B such that

$$(A_1 A_2 \cdots A_n) B = I$$

where B is the inverse matrix of the product. To remove A_1 from the product, we can then write

$$A_1^{-1}(A_1 A_2 \cdots A_n) B = A_1^{-1} I$$

which would reduce the equation to

$$(A_2 A_3 \cdots A_n) B = A_1^{-1} I.$$

Likewise, then, from

$$A_2^{-1}(A_2 A_3 \cdots A_n) B = A_2^{-1} A_1^{-1} I$$

which simplifies to

$$(A_3 A_4 \cdots A_n) B = A_2^{-1} A_1^{-1} I.$$

If one repeat the process up to A_n, the equation becomes

$$B = A_n^{-1} A_{n-1}^{-1} \cdots A_2^{-1} A_1^{-1} I$$

$$B = A_n^{-1} A_{n-1}^{-1} \cdots A_2^{-1} A_1^{-1}$$

but B is the inverse matrix, i.e. $B = (A_1 A_2 \cdots A_n)^{-1}$ so the property is established.

Over the field of real numbers, the set of singular n-by-n matrices, considered as a subset of $R^{n \times n}$, is a null set, i.e., has Lebesgue measure zero.

   a. -module
   b. 2-bridge knot
   c. -equivalence
   d. Nonsingular

8. In its simplest meaning in mathematics and logic, an _____ is an action or procedure which produces a new value from one or more input values. There are two common types of operations: unary and binary. Unary operations involve only one value, such as negation and trigonometric functions.
   a. Abelian P-root group
   b. Operation
   c. ADE classification
   d. AKS primality test

9. In mathematics, a _____ is a constant multiplicative factor of a certain object. For example, in the expression $9x^2$, the _____ of x^2 is 9.

The object can be such things as a variable, a vector, a function, etc.

   a. Constant term
   b. Vandermonde polynomial
   c. Tschirnhaus transformation
   d. Coefficient

10. In mathematics, an _____ is a simple matrix which differs from the identity matrix in a minimal way. The elementary matrices generate the general linear group of invertible matrices, and left (respectively, right) multiplication by an _____ represent elementary row operations (respectively, elementary column operations.)

In algebraic K-theory, 'elementary matrices' refers only to the row-addition matrices.

   a. Orientation
   b. Elementary matrix
   c. Orthogonalization
   d. Orthonormal basis

11. In linear algebra, the _____ or unit matrix of size n is the n-by-n square matrix with ones on the main diagonal and zeros elsewhere. It is denoted by I_n, or simply by I if the size is immaterial or can be trivially determined by the context. (In some fields, such as quantum mechanics, the _____ is denoted by a boldface one, 1; otherwise it is identical to I.)

   a. Identity matrix
   b. Associativity
   c. Orthogonal
   d. Artinian ideal

12. In mathematics, a _____ is a rectangular array of numbers. This way, matrices can record data that depend on multiple parameters. In particular they are used to keep track of the coefficients of multiple linear equations. Matrices are closely connected to linear transformations, which are higher-dimensional analogs of linear functions, i.e., functions of the form $f(x) = c · x$, where c is a constant. This map corresponds to a _____ with one row and column, with entry c. In addition to a number of elementary, entrywise operations such as _____ addition a key notion is _____ multiplication, which displays a number of features not encountered in numbers; for example, products of matrices depend on the order of the factors, unlike products of real numbers, say, where $c · d = d · c$ for any two numbers c and d.

a. Heap
b. Polynomial expression
c. Commutativity
d. Matrix

13. In the mathematical discipline of linear algebra, a _____ is a special kind of square matrix where the entries either below or above the main diagonal are zero. Because matrix equations with triangular matrices are easier to solve they are very important in numerical analysis. The LU decomposition gives an algorithm to decompose any invertible matrix A into a normed lower triangle matrix L and an upper triangle matrix U.
   a. Hilbert matrix
   b. Circulant matrix
   c. Diagonally dominant
   d. Triangular matrix

14. In linear algebra, a _____ matrix is a square matrix A whose transpose is also its negative; that is, it satisfies the equation:

$$A^T = -A$$

or in component form, if $A = (a_{ij})$:

$$a_{ij} = -a_{ji} \text{ for all } i \text{ and } j.$$

For example, the following matrix is _____:

$$\begin{bmatrix} 0 & 2 & -1 \\ -2 & 0 & -4 \\ 1 & 4 & 0 \end{bmatrix}.$$

Compare this with a symmetric matrix whose transpose is the same as the matrix

$$A^T = A,$$

or to an orthogonal matrix, the transpose of which is equal to its inverse:

$$A^T = A^{-1}.$$

Sums and scalar products of _____ matrices are again _____. Hence, the _____ matrices form a vector space. Its dimension is $\frac{n(n-1)}{2}$.

a. Complex Hadamard matrix
b. Bisymmetric matrix
c. Duplication matrix
d. Skew-symmetric

15. _____ is called _____ matrix or right triangular matrix.

The standard operations on triangular matrices conveniently preserve the triangular form: the sum and product of two _____ matrices is again _____. The inverse of an _____ matrix is also _____, and of course we can multiply an _____ matrix by a constant and it will still be _____.

a. Upper triangular
b. Abelian P-root group
c. ADE classification
d. AKS primality test

16. In mathematics, a _____ is a semigroup in which every element is idempotent The lattice of varieties of bands was described independently by Birjukov, Fennemore and Gerhard. Semilattices, left-zero bands, right-zero bands, rectangular bands and regular bands, specific subclasses of bands which lie near the bottom of this lattice, are of particular interest and are briefly described below.
a. Direct product
b. Formal power series
c. Group extension
d. Band

17. In mathematics, particularly matrix theory, a _____ is a sparse matrix, whose non-zero entries are confined to a diagonal band, comprising the main diagonal and zero or more diagonals on either side.

Formally, an n×n matrix A=($a_{i,j}$) is a _____ if all matrix elements are zero outside a diagonally bordered band whose range is determined by constants k_1 and k_2:

$$a_{i,j} = 0 \quad \text{if} \quad j < i - k_1 \quad \text{or} \quad j > i + k_2; \quad k_1, k_2 \geq 0.$$

The quantities k_1 and k_2 are the left and right half-bandwidth, respectively. The bandwidth of the matrix is $k_1 + k_2 + 1$ (in other words, the smallest number of adjacent diagonals to which the non-zero elements are confined.)

  a. Modal matrix
  b. Skew-symmetric
  c. Binary matrix
  d. Band matrix

18. In several fields of mathematics the term _____ is used with different but closely related meanings. They all relate to the notion of mapping the elements of a set to other elements of the same set, i.e., exchanging (or 'permuting') elements of a set.

The general concept of _____ can be defined more formally in different contexts:

In combinatorics, a _____ is usually understood to be a sequence containing each element from a finite set once, and only once.

  a. Permutation
  b. Rupture field
  c. Near-field
  d. Binary function

19. In mathematics, in matrix theory, a _____ is a square (0,1)-matrix that has exactly one entry 1 in each row and each column and 0's elsewhere. Each such matrix represents a specific permutation of m elements and, when used to multiply another matrix, can produce that permutation in the rows or columns of the other matrix.

Given a permutation π of m elements,

$$\pi : \{1, \ldots, m\} \to \{1, \ldots, m\}$$

given in two-line form by

$$\begin{pmatrix} 1 & 2 & \cdots & m \\ \pi(1) & \pi(2) & \cdots & \pi(m) \end{pmatrix},$$

its _____ is the m × m matrix P_π whose entries are all 0 except that in row i, the entry π(i) equals 1.

Chapter 1. MATRICES AND GAUSSIAN ELIMINATION

a. Hessenberg matrix
b. Skew-symmetric
c. Main diagonal
d. Permutation matrix

20. Let S be a set with a binary operation * . If e is an identity element of (S, *) and a * b = e, then a is called a _____ of b and b is called a right inverse of a. If an element x is both a _____ and a right inverse of y, then x is called a two-sided inverse, or simply an inverse, of y.
    a. 2-bridge knot
    b. -module
    c. -equivalence
    d. Left inverse

21. In linear algebra, the _____ of a matrix A is another matrix A^T (also written A', A^{tr} or ^tA) created by any one of the following equivalent actions:

    - write the rows of A as the columns of A^T
    - write the columns of A as the rows of A^T
    - reflect A by its main diagonal (which starts from the top left) to obtain A^T

    Formally, the _____ of an m × n matrix A with elements A_{ij} is the n × m matrix

    $$A^T_{ij} = A_{ji} \text{ for } 1 \leq i \leq n, 1 \leq j \leq m.$$

    The _____ of a scalar is the same scalar.

    - $\begin{bmatrix} 1 & 2 \end{bmatrix}^T = \begin{bmatrix} 1 \\ 2 \end{bmatrix}.$

    - $\begin{bmatrix} 1 & 2 \\ 3 & 4 \end{bmatrix}^T = \begin{bmatrix} 1 & 3 \\ 2 & 4 \end{bmatrix}.$

    - $\begin{bmatrix} 1 & 2 \\ 3 & 4 \\ 5 & 6 \end{bmatrix}^T = \begin{bmatrix} 1 & 3 & 5 \\ 2 & 4 & 6 \end{bmatrix}.$

For matrices A, B and scalar c we have the following properties of _____:

1. $\left(\mathbf{A}^T\right)^T = \mathbf{A}$

   Taking the _____ is an involution (self inverse.)

- $(\mathbf{A}+\mathbf{B})^T = \mathbf{A}^T + \mathbf{B}^T$

   The _____ respects addition.

- $(\mathbf{AB})^T = \mathbf{B}^T\mathbf{A}^T$

   Note that the order of the factors reverses. From this one can deduce that a square matrix A is invertible if and only if A^T is invertible, and in this case we have $(A^{-1})^T = (A^T)^{-1}$. It is relatively easy to extend this result to the general case of multiple matrices, where we find that $(ABC...XYZ)^T = Z^T Y^T X^T ...C^T B^T A^T$.

- $(c\mathbf{A})^T = c\mathbf{A}^T$

   The _____ of a scalar is the same scalar. Together with (2), this states that the _____ is a linear map from the space of m × n matrices to the space of all n × m matrices.

- $\det(\mathbf{A}^T) = \det(\mathbf{A})$

   The determinant of a square matrix is the same as that of its _____.

- The dot product of two column vectors a and b can be computed as

   $$\mathbf{a} \cdot \mathbf{b} = \mathbf{a}^T \mathbf{b},$$

   which is written as $a_i b^i$ in Einstein notation.
- If A has only real entries, then $A^T A$ is a positive-semidefinite matrix.
- $\left(\mathbf{A}^T\right)^{-1} = \left(\mathbf{A}^{-1}\right)^T$

   The _____ of an invertible matrix is also invertible, and its inverse is the _____ of the inverse of the original matrix.

- If A is a square matrix, then its eigenvalues are equal to the eigenvalues of its _____.

A square matrix whose _____ is equal to itself is called a symmetric matrix; that is, A is symmetric if

$$\mathbf{A}^T = \mathbf{A}.$$

A square matrix whose _____ is also its inverse is called an orthogonal matrix; that is, G is orthogonal if

$$\mathbf{G}\mathbf{G}^T = \mathbf{G}^T\mathbf{G} = \mathbf{I}_n,$$ the identity matrix, i.e. $G^T = G^{-1}$.

A square matrix whose _____ is equal to its negative is called skew-symmetric matrix; that is, A is skew-symmetric if

$$\mathbf{A}^T = -\mathbf{A}.$$

The conjugate _____ of the complex matrix A, written as A^*, is obtained by taking the _____ of A and the complex conjugate of each entry:

$$\mathbf{A}^* = (\overline{\mathbf{A}})^T = \overline{(\mathbf{A}^T)}.$$

If f: V→W is a linear map between vector spaces V and W with nondegenerate bilinear forms, we define the _____ of f to be the linear map $^t f$: W→V, determined by

$$B_V(v, {}^t f(w)) = B_W(f(v), w) \quad \forall\ v \in V, w \in W.$$

Here, B_V and B_W are the bilinear forms on V and W respectively. The matrix of the _____ of a map is the transposed matrix only if the bases are orthonormal with respect to their bilinear forms.

Over a complex vector space, one often works with sesquilinear forms instead of bilinear (conjugate-linear in one argument.)

a. Tridiagonal matrix
b. Drazin inverse
c. Levinson recursion
d. Transpose

22. In the case of Gaussian elimination, it is best to choose a pivot element with large absolute value. This improves the numerical stability. In _____, the algorithm considers all entries in the column of the matrix that is currently being considered, picks the entry with largest absolute value, and finally swaps rows such that this entry is the pivot in question.

a. -module
b. 2-bridge knot
c. -equivalence
d. Partial pivoting

23. A _____ is a set G closed under a binary operation · satisfying the following 3 axioms:

- Associativity: For all a, b and c in G, (a · b) · c = a · (b · c.)
- Identity element: There exists an e∈G such that for all a in G, e · a = a · e = a.
- Inverse element: For each a in G, there is an element b in G such that a · b = b · a = e, where e is an identity element.

Basic examples for groups are the integers Z with addition operation, or rational numbers without zero Q{0} with multiplication. More generally, for any ring R, the units in R form a multiplicative _____ Groups include, however, much more general structures than the above.

a. Group
b. Nilpotent group
c. Grigorchuk group
d. Product of group subsets

Chapter 2. VECTOR SPACES AND LINEAR EQUATIONS

1. In linear algebra, the _____ of a matrix is the set of all possible linear combinations of its column vectors. The _____ of an m × n matrix is a subspace of m-dimensional Euclidean space. The dimension of the _____ is called the rank of the matrix.
   a. Column space
   b. Delta operator
   c. Pseudovector
   d. Linear inequality

2. If $A_1, A_2, ..., A_n$ are _____ square matrices over a field, then

$$(A_1 A_2 \cdots A_n)^{-1} = A_n^{-1} A_{n-1}^{-1} \cdots A_1^{-1}.$$

It becomes evident why this is the case if one attempts to find an inverse for the product of the A_is from first principles, that is, that we wish to determine B such that

$$(A_1 A_2 \cdots A_n) B = I$$

where B is the inverse matrix of the product. To remove A_1 from the product, we can then write

$$A_1^{-1}(A_1 A_2 \cdots A_n) B = A_1^{-1} I$$

which would reduce the equation to

$$(A_2 A_3 \cdots A_n) B = A_1^{-1} I.$$

Likewise, then, from

$$A_2^{-1}(A_2 A_3 \cdots A_n) B = A_2^{-1} A_1^{-1} I$$

which simplifies to

$$(A_3 A_4 \cdots A_n) B = A_2^{-1} A_1^{-1} I.$$

If one repeat the process up to A_n, the equation becomes

$$B = A_n^{-1} A_{n-1}^{-1} \cdots A_2^{-1} A_1^{-1} I$$

$$B = A_n^{-1} A_{n-1}^{-1} \cdots A_2^{-1} A_1^{-1}$$

Chapter 2. VECTOR SPACES AND LINEAR EQUATIONS

but B is the inverse matrix, i.e. $B = (A_1 A_2 \cdots A_n)^{-1}$ so the property is established.

Over the field of real numbers, the set of singular n-by-n matrices, considered as a subset of $R^{n \times n}$, is a null set, i.e., has Lebesgue measure zero.

a. -module
b. Nonsingular
c. -equivalence
d. 2-bridge knot

3. In mathematics, _____ or factoring is the decomposition of an object ' href='/wiki/Matrix_(mathematics)'>matrix) into a product of other objects, or factors, which when multiplied together give the original. For example, the number 15 factors into primes as 3 × 5, and the polynomial x^2 − 4 factors as (x − 2)(x + 2.) In all cases, a product of simpler objects is obtained.

a. -module
b. 2-bridge knot
c. -equivalence
d. Factorization

4. A _____ is a symbol that stands for a value that may vary; the term usually occurs in opposition to constant, which is a symbol for a non-varying value, i.e. completely fixed or fixed in the context of use. The concepts of constants and variables are fundamental to all modern mathematics, science, engineering, and computer programming.

Much of the basic theory for which we use variables today, such as school geometry and algebra, was developed thousands of years ago, but the use of symbolic formulae and variables is only several hundreds of years old.

a. -equivalence
b. -module
c. 2-bridge knot
d. Variable

5. In mathematics, there are several meanings of _____ depending on the subject.

A _____, usually denoted by ° (the _____ symbol), is a measurement of plane angle, representing $1/360$ of a full rotation. When that angle is with respect to a reference meridian, it indicates a location along a great circle of a sphere, such as Earth , Mars, or the celestial sphere.

Chapter 2. VECTOR SPACES AND LINEAR EQUATIONS

a. Relation algebra
b. Median algebra
c. Symmetric difference
d. Degree

6. In mathematics, the _____ of a vector space V is the cardinality (i.e. the number of vectors) of a basis of V. It is sometimes called Hamel _____ or algebraic _____ to distinguish it from other types of _____. All bases of a vector space have equal cardinality and so the _____ of a vector space is uniquely defined. The _____ of the vector space V over the field F can be written as $\dim_F(V)$ or as [V : F], read '_____ of V over F'.

a. Partial trace
b. Dual basis
c. Cofactor
d. Dimension

7. The column _____ of a matrix A is the maximal number of linearly independent columns of A. Likewise, the row _____ is the maximal number of linearly independent rows of A.

Since the column _____ and the row _____ are always equal, they are simply called the _____ of A. More abstractly, it is the dimension of the image of A. For the proofs, see, e.g., Murase (1960), Andrea ' Wong (1960), Williams ' Cater (1968), Mackiw (1995).) It is commonly denoted by either rk(A) or _____ A.

a. Split-complex number
b. Schur complement
c. Generalized Pauli matrices
d. Rank

8. In mathematics, a _____ is a rectangular array of numbers. This way, matrices can record data that depend on multiple parameters. In particular they are used to keep track of the coefficients of multiple linear equations. Matrices are closely connected to linear transformations, which are higher-dimensional analogs of linear functions, i.e., functions of the form f(x) = c Â· x, where c is a constant. This map corresponds to a _____ with one row and column, with entry c. In addition to a number of elementary, entrywise operations such as _____ addition a key notion is _____ multiplication, which displays a number of features not encountered in numbers; for example, products of matrices depend on the order of the factors, unlike products of real numbers, say, where c Â· d = d Â· c for any two numbers c and d.

a. Commutativity
b. Matrix
c. Heap
d. Polynomial expression

Chapter 2. VECTOR SPACES AND LINEAR EQUATIONS

9. In linear algebra, a family of vectors is _____ if none of them can be written as a linear combination of finitely many other vectors in the collection. A family of vectors which is not _____ is called linearly dependent. For instance, in the three-dimensional real vector space $\mathbb{R}^3$ we have the following example.
   a. Linearly independent
   b. Composition ring
   c. Grothendieck group
   d. Derivative algebra

10. The _____ of an m-by-n matrix with real entries is the subspace of R^n generated by the row vectors of the matrix. Its dimension is equal to the rank of the matrix and is at most min(m,n.)

The column space of an m-by-n matrix with real entries is the subspace of R^m generated by the column vectors of the matrix.

   a. Differential graded algebra
   b. Goodman-Nguyen-van Fraassen algebra
   c. Restriction of scalars
   d. Row space

11. In the various branches of mathematics that fall under the heading of abstract algebra, the _____ of a homomorphism measures the degree to which the homomorphism fails to be injective. An important special case is the _____ of a matrix, also called the null space.

The definition of _____ takes various forms in various contexts.

   a. K-theory
   b. Completing the square
   c. Monomial basis
   d. Kernel

12. In mathematics, an _____ is a matrix that shows the relationship between two classes of objects. If the first class is X and the second is Y, the matrix has one row for each element of X and one column for each element of Y. The entry in row x and column y is 1 if x and y are related (called incident in this context) and 0 if they are not.
   a. Abelian P-root group
   b. AKS primality test
   c. ADE classification
   d. Incidence matrix

Chapter 2. VECTOR SPACES AND LINEAR EQUATIONS

13. The method of _____ is used to approximately solve overdetermined systems, i.e. systems of equations in which there are more equations than unknowns. _____ is often applied in statistical contexts, particularly regression analysis.

   _____ can be interpreted as a method of fitting data.

   a. -module
   b. 2-bridge knot
   c. Least squares
   d. -equivalence

14. In linear algebra, a _____ is a linear transformation that squares to the identity ($R^2 = I$, where R is in K dimensional space), also known as an involution in the general linear group. In addition to reflections across hyperplanes, the class of general reflections includes point reflections, reflections across subspaces of intermediate dimension, and non-orthogonal reflections.

   A _____ over a hyperplane in an inner product space is necessarily symmetric, but a general _____ need not be as the example $\begin{bmatrix} 1 & 0 \\ 1 & -1 \end{bmatrix}$ shows.

   a. Homomorphic secret sharing
   b. Shear mappings
   c. Reflection
   d. Morphism

15. In geometry and linear algebra, a _____ is a transformation in a plane or in space that describes the motion of a rigid body around a fixed point. A _____ is different from a translation, which has no fixed points, and from a reflection, which 'flips' the bodies it is transforming. A _____ and the above-mentioned transformations are isometries; they leave the distance between any two points unchanged after the transformation.

   a. Real matrices
   b. Reflection
   c. Shear mappings
   d. Rotation

16. In linear algebra and functional analysis, a _____ is a linear transformation P from a vector space to itself such that $P^2 = P$. It leaves its image unchanged. Though abstract, this definition of '_____' formalizes and generalizes the idea of graphical _____.

Chapter 2. VECTOR SPACES AND LINEAR EQUATIONS

a. C_0-semigroup
b. Lumer-Phillips theorem
c. Convolution power
d. Projection

17. In linear algebra, a basis for a vector space of dimension n is a sequence of n vectors $a_1, ..., a_n$ with the property that every vector in the space can be expressed uniquely as a linear combination of the basis vectors. Since it is often desirable to work with more than one basis for a vector space, it is of fundamental importance in linear algebra to be able to easily transform coordinate-wise representations of vectors and linear transformations taken with respect to one basis to their equivalent representations with respect to another basis. Such a transformation is called a _____.

a. Generalized singular value decomposition
b. Split-complex number
c. Change of basis
d. Field of values

18. In linear algebra, a _____ is a set of vectors that, in a linear combination, can represent every vector in a given vector space or free module, and such that no element of the set can be represented as a linear combination of the others. In other words, a _____ is a linearly independent spanning set.

a. Minor
b. Chirality
c. Basis
d. Supergroup

19. In several fields of mathematics the term _____ is used with different but closely related meanings. They all relate to the notion of mapping the elements of a set to other elements of the same set, i.e., exchanging (or 'permuting') elements of a set.

The general concept of _____ can be defined more formally in different contexts:

In combinatorics, a _____ is usually understood to be a sequence containing each element from a finite set once, and only once.

a. Permutation
b. Near-field
c. Rupture field
d. Binary function

Chapter 3. ORTHOGONALITY

1. In abstract algebra, the _____ of a module is a measure of the module's 'size'. It is defined as the _____ of the longest ascending chain of submodules and is a generalization of the concept of dimension for vector spaces. The modules with finite _____ share many important properties with finite-dimensional vector spaces.
    a. Length
    b. Finitely generated module
    c. Morita equivalence
    d. Supermodule

2. In mathematics, two vectors are _____ if they are perpendicular, i.e., they form a right angle. The word comes from the Greek ὀρθός, meaning 'straight', and γωνία (gonia), meaning 'angle'. For example, a subway and the street above, although they do not physically intersect, are _____ if they cross at a right angle.
    a. Unital
    b. Embedding
    c. Expression
    d. Orthogonal

3. In geometry, two lines or planes (or a line and a plane), are considered _____ to each other if they form congruent adjacent angles (an L-shape.) The term may be used as a noun or adjective. Thus, referring to Figure 1, the line AB is the _____ to CD through the point B. Note that by definition, a line is infinitely long, and strictly speaking AB and CD in this example represent line segments of two infinitely long lines.
    a. Perpendicular
    b. -equivalence
    c. -module
    d. 2-bridge knot

4. In linear algebra, two vectors in an inner product space are _____ if they are orthogonal and both of unit length. A set of vectors form an _____ set if all vectors in the set are mutually orthogonal and all of unit length. An _____ set which forms a basis is called an _____ basis.
    a. Invertible matrix
    b. Orthonormal
    c. Elementary matrix
    d. Overdetermined

5. In linear algebra, the _____ of a matrix is the set of all possible linear combinations of its column vectors. The _____ of an m × n matrix is a subspace of m-dimensional Euclidean space. The dimension of the _____ is called the rank of the matrix.

a. Delta operator
b. Linear inequality
c. Pseudovector
d. Column space

6. The _____ of an m-by-n matrix with real entries is the subspace of R^n generated by the row vectors of the matrix. Its dimension is equal to the rank of the matrix and is at most min(m,n.)

The column space of an m-by-n matrix with real entries is the subspace of R^m generated by the column vectors of the matrix.

a. Goodman-Nguyen-van Fraassen algebra
b. Differential graded algebra
c. Restriction of scalars
d. Row space

7. In discrete mathematics and predominantly in set theory, a _____ is a concept used in comparisons of sets to refer to the unique values of one set in relation to another. The terms 'absolute' and 'relative' _____ refer to more specific applications of the concept, with universal complements referring to elements unique to the universal set and the latter referring to the unique elements of one set in relation to another. In this image, the universal set is represented by the border of the image, and the set A as a disc.
a. -equivalence
b. Complement
c. -module
d. Pointed set

8. In the mathematical fields of linear algebra and functional analysis, the _____ $W^\perp$ of a subspace W of an inner product space V is the set of all vectors in V that are orthogonal to every vector in W, i.e., it is

$$W^\perp = \{x \in V : \langle x, y \rangle = 0 \text{ for all } y \in W\}.$$

Informally, it is called the perp, short for perpendicular complement.

The _____ is always closed in the metric topology. In finite-dimensional spaces, that is merely an instance of the fact that all subspaces of a vector space are closed.

a. Invariant subspace
b. Euclidean subspace
c. Orthogonal complement
d. Independent equation

9. In mathematics, in particular functional analysis, the _____, or s-numbers of a compact operator T acting on a Hilbert space are defined as the eigenvalues of the operator $\sqrt{T^*T}$ (where T* denotes the adjoint of T and the square root is taken in the operator sense.) The _____ are nonnegative real numbers, usually listed in decreasing order $s_1(T)$, $s_2(T)$, ...
   a. 2-bridge knot
   b. -module
   c. -equivalence
   d. Singular values

10. In linear algebra, the _____ is an important factorization of a rectangular real or complex matrix, with several applications in signal processing and statistics. Applications which employ the _____ include computing the pseudoinverse, least squares fitting of data, matrix approximation, and determining the rank, range and null space of a matrix.

Suppose M is an m-by-n matrix whose entries come from the field K, which is either the field of real numbers or the field of complex numbers.

   a. -module
   b. -equivalence
   c. 2-bridge knot
   d. Singular value decomposition

11. In linear algebra and functional analysis, a _____ is a linear transformation P from a vector space to itself such that $P^2 = P$. It leaves its image unchanged. Though abstract, this definition of '_____' formalizes and generalizes the idea of graphical _____.
   a. C_0-semigroup
   b. Lumer-Phillips theorem
   c. Convolution power
   d. Projection

12. The _____ of an angle is the ratio of the length of the adjacent side to the length of the hypotenuse. In our case

$$\cos A = \frac{\text{adjacent}}{\text{hypotenuse}} = \frac{b}{h}.$$

The tangent of an angle is the ratio of the length of the opposite side to the length of the adjacent side. In our case

$$\tan A = \frac{\text{opposite}}{\text{adjacent}} = \frac{a}{b}.$$

The remaining three functions are best defined using the above three functions.

a. -module
b. Cosine
c. -equivalence
d. 2-bridge knot

13. In mathematics, a system of linear equations is considered _____ if there are more equations than unknowns. The terminology can be described in terms of the concept of counting constants. Each unknown can be seen as an available degree of freedom.
 a. Euclidean subspace
 b. Orthogonalization
 c. Elementary matrix
 d. Overdetermined

14. In mathematics, the Cauchy-_____ the Cauchy inequality is a useful inequality encountered in many different settings, such as linear algebra applied to vectors, in analysis applied to infinite series and integration of products, and in probability theory, applied to variances and covariances. The general formulation of the Heisenberg uncertainty principle is derived using the Cauchy-_____ in the Hilbert space of pure quantum states.

The inequality for sums was published by , while the corresponding inequality for integrals was first stated by and rediscovered by

 a. -equivalence
 b. -module
 c. 2-bridge knot
 d. Schwarz inequality

15. In mathematics, an _____ is a statement about the relative size or order of two objects, or about whether they are the same or not

- The notation a < b means that a is less than b.
- The notation a > b means that a is greater than b.
- The notation a ≠ b means that a is not equal to b, but does not say that one is bigger than the other or even that they can be compared in size.

In all these cases, a is not equal to b, hence, '_____'.

These relations are known as strict _____

- The notation a ≤ b means that a is less than or equal to b (or, equivalently, not greater than b);
- The notation a ≥ b means that a is greater than or equal to b (or, equivalently, not smaller than b);

An additional use of the notation is to show that one quantity is much greater than another, normally by several orders of magnitude.

- The notation a ≪ b means that a is much less than b.
- The notation a ≫ b means that a is much greater than b.

If the sense of the _____ is the same for all values of the variables for which its members are defined, then the _____ is called an 'absolute' or 'unconditional' _____. If the sense of an _____ holds only for certain values of the variables involved, but is reversed or destroyed for other values of the variables, it is called a conditional _____.

One can apply the same algebraic operations to inequalities as one would apply for solving equalities. For example, to find x for the _____ 10x > 20 one would divide 20 by 10 to obtain x > 2.

a. ADE classification
b. Abelian P-root group
c. Inequality
d. AKS primality test

16. In algebra, a commutative ring R is said to be _____ if any of the following equivalent conditions holds:

1. The localization $R_\mathfrak{m}$ of R at $\mathfrak{m}$ is a valuation ring for every maximal ideal $\mathfrak{m}$ of R.
2. For all ideals $\mathfrak{a}$, $\mathfrak{b}$, and $\mathfrak{c}$,

$$\mathfrak{a} \cap (\mathfrak{b} + \mathfrak{c}) = (\mathfrak{a} \cap \mathfrak{b}) + (\mathfrak{a} \cap \mathfrak{c})$$

- For all ideals $\mathfrak{a}$, $\mathfrak{b}$, and $\mathfrak{c}$,

$$a + (b \cap c) = (a + b) \cap (a + c)$$

An _____ domain is called a Prüfer domain.

  a. Exchange matrix
  b. Ordered vector space
  c. Arithmetical
  d. Inverse eigenvalues theorem

17. In mathematics, a _____ is a rectangular array of numbers. This way, matrices can record data that depend on multiple parameters. In particular they are used to keep track of the coefficients of multiple linear equations. Matrices are closely connected to linear transformations, which are higher-dimensional analogs of linear functions, i.e., functions of the form f(x) = c Â· x, where c is a constant. This map corresponds to a _____ with one row and column, with entry c. In addition to a number of elementary, entrywise operations such as _____ addition a key notion is _____ multiplication, which displays a number of features not encountered in numbers; for example, products of matrices depend on the order of the factors, unlike products of real numbers, say, where c Â· d = d Â· c for any two numbers c and d.
  a. Heap
  b. Polynomial expression
  c. Matrix
  d. Commutativity

18. In linear algebra, the _____ of an n-by-n square matrix A is defined to be the sum of the elements on the main diagonal (the diagonal from the upper left to the lower right) of A, i.e.,

$$\operatorname{tr}(A) = a_{11} + a_{22} + \cdots + a_{nn} = \sum_{i=1}^{n} a_{ii}$$

where a_{ij} represents the entry on the ith row and jth column of A. Equivalently, the _____ of a matrix is the sum of its eigenvalues, making it an invariant with respect to a change of basis. This characterization can be used to define the _____ for a linear operator in general.

Note that the _____ is only defined for a square matrix (i.e. n×n.)

  a. Coefficient matrix
  b. Dot product
  c. Trace
  d. Defective matrix

Chapter 3. ORTHOGONALITY

19. A _____ is one of the basic shapes of geometry: a polygon with three corners or vertices and three sides or edges which are line segments. A _____ with vertices A, B, and C is denoted ABC.

In Euclidean geometry any three non-collinear points determine a unique _____ and a unique plane (i.e. a two-dimensional Euclidean space.)

   a. -module
   b. -equivalence
   c. 2-bridge knot
   d. Triangle

20. In mathematics, the _____ states that for any triangle, the length of a given side must be less than the sum of the other two sides but greater than the difference between the two sides.

In Euclidean geometry and some other geometries this is a theorem. In the Euclidean case, in both the less than or equal to and greater than or equal to statements, equality occurs only if the triangle has a 180° angle and two 0° angles, as shown in the bottom example in the image to the right.

   a. 2-bridge knot
   b. -equivalence
   c. -module
   d. Triangle inequality

21. _____ is a concept that permeates much of inferential statistics and descriptive statistics. More properly, it is 'the sum of the squared deviations'. Mathematically, it is an unscaled, or unadjusted measure of dispersion (also called variability.)
   a. -equivalence
   b. 2-bridge knot
   c. -module
   d. Sum of squares

22. The method of _____ is used to approximately solve overdetermined systems, i.e. systems of equations in which there are more equations than unknowns. _____ is often applied in statistical contexts, particularly regression analysis.

_____ can be interpreted as a method of fitting data.

Chapter 3. ORTHOGONALITY

a. -equivalence
b. -module
c. 2-bridge knot
d. Least squares

23. The _____ magnitude or Error vectorM is a measure used to quantify the performance of a digital radio transmitter or receiver. A signal sent by an ideal transmitter or received by a receiver would have all constellation points precisely at the ideal locations, however various imperfections in the implementation cause the actual constellation points to deviate from the ideal locations.
   a. AKS primality test
   b. Abelian P-root group
   c. Error vector
   d. ADE classification

24. In geometry, a _____ is a straight curve. When geometry is used to model the real world, lines are used to represent straight objects with negligible width and height. Lines are an idealisation of such objects and have no width or height at all and are usually considered to be infinitely long.
   a. 2-bridge knot
   b. Line
   c. -equivalence
   d. -module

25. In linear algebra, a _____ is a linear transformation that squares to the identity ($R^2 = I$, where R is in K dimensional space), also known as an involution in the general linear group. In addition to reflections across hyperplanes, the class of general reflections includes point reflections, reflections across subspaces of intermediate dimension, and non-orthogonal reflections.

A _____ over a hyperplane in an inner product space is necessarily symmetric, but a general _____ need not be as the example $\begin{bmatrix} 1 & 0 \\ 1 & -1 \end{bmatrix}$ shows.

   a. Homomorphic secret sharing
   b. Shear mappings
   c. Morphism
   d. Reflection

26. In mathematics, the _____ for a Euclidean space consists of one unit vector pointing in the direction of each axis of the Cartesian coordinate system. For example, the _____ for the Euclidean plane are the vectors

$$\mathbf{e}_x = (1,0), \quad \mathbf{e}_y = (0,1),$$

and the _____ for three-dimensional space are the vectors

$$\mathbf{e}_x = (1,0,0), \quad \mathbf{e}_y = (0,1,0), \quad \mathbf{e}_z = (0,0,1).$$

Here the vector e_x points in the x direction, the vector e_y points in the y direction, and the vector e_z points in the z direction. There are several common notations for these vectors, including {e_x, e_y, e_z}, {e_1, e_2, e_3}, {i, j, k}, and {x, y, z}.

a. 2-bridge knot
b. -module
c. -equivalence
d. Standard basis

27. In mathematics, a _____ in a (unital) ring R is an invertible element of R, i.e. an element u such that there is a v in R with

uv = vu = 1_R, where 1_R is the multiplicative identity element.

That is, u is an invertible element of the multiplicative monoid of R. If $0 \neq 1$ in the ring, then 0 is not a _____.

Unfortunately, the term _____ is also used to refer to the identity element 1_R of the ring, in expressions like ring with a _____ or _____ ring, and also e.g. '_____' matrix.

a. Ore extension
b. Unit
c. Ascending chain condition on principal ideals
d. Ore condition

28. In linear algebra, a _____ is a set of vectors that, in a linear combination, can represent every vector in a given vector space or free module, and such that no element of the set can be represented as a linear combination of the others. In other words, a _____ is a linearly independent spanning set.

a. Basis
b. Minor
c. Chirality
d. Supergroup

29. In linear algebra, an _____ is a square matrix with real entries whose columns (or rows) are orthogonal unit vectors (i.e., orthonormal.) Equivalently, a matrix Q is orthogonal if its transpose is equal to its inverse:

$$Q^T Q = QQ^T = I.$$

As a linear transformation, an _____ preserves the dot product of vectors, and therefore acts as an isometry of Euclidean space, such as a rotation or reflection.

The set of n × n orthogonal matrices forms a group O(n), known as the orthogonal group.

a. Orthogonal matrix
b. Unimodular matrix
c. Alternating sign matrix
d. Unistochastic matrix

30. In geometry and linear algebra, a _____ is a transformation in a plane or in space that describes the motion of a rigid body around a fixed point. A _____ is different from a translation, which has no fixed points, and from a reflection, which 'flips' the bodies it is transforming. A _____ and the above-mentioned transformations are isometries; they leave the distance between any two points unchanged after the transformation.

a. Rotation
b. Shear mappings
c. Reflection
d. Real matrices

31. In mathematics, a _____ decomposes a periodic function or periodic signal into a sum of simple oscillating functions, namely sines and cosines . The study of _____ is a branch of Fourier analysis. _____ were introduced by Joseph Fourier (1768-1830) for the purpose of solving the heat equation in a metal plate.

a. Fourier series
b. 2-bridge knot
c. -equivalence
d. -module

32. In linear algebra, _____ is the process of finding a set of orthogonal vectors that span a particular subspace. Formally, starting with a linearly independent set of vectors $\{v_1,...,v_k\}$ in an inner product space (most commonly the Euclidean space R^n), _____ results in a set of orthogonal vectors $\{u_1,...,u_k\}$ that generate the same subspace as the vectors $v_1,...,v_k$. Every vector in the new set is orthogonal to every other vector in the new set; and the new set and the old set have the same linear span.
   a. Independent equation
   b. Orthogonal Procrustes problem
   c. Orthonormal
   d. Orthogonalization

33. In mathematics, _____ or factoring is the decomposition of an object ' href='/wiki/Matrix_(mathematics)'>matrix) into a product of other objects, or factors, which when multiplied together give the original. For example, the number 15 factors into primes as 3 × 5, and the polynomial $x^2 - 4$ factors as $(x - 2)(x + 2)$. In all cases, a product of simpler objects is obtained.
   a. 2-bridge knot
   b. Factorization
   c. -equivalence
   d. -module

34. An _____ is a type of quadric surface that is a higher dimensional analogue of an ellipse. The equation of a standard axis-aligned _____ body in an xyz-Cartesian coordinate system is

$$\frac{x^2}{a^2} + \frac{y^2}{b^2} + \frac{z^2}{c^2} = 1$$

where a and b are the equatorial radii (along the x and y axes) and c is the polar radius (along the z-axis), all of which are fixed positive real numbers determining the shape of the _____.

More generally, a not-necessarily-axis-aligned _____ is defined by the equation

$$\mathbf{x}^T A \mathbf{x} = 1$$

where A is a symmetric positive definite matrix and x is a vector.

   a. ADE classification
   b. AKS primality test
   c. Abelian P-root group
   d. Ellipsoid

Chapter 3. ORTHOGONALITY

35. In mathematics, the complex numbers are an extension of the real numbers obtained by adjoining an imaginary unit, denoted i, which satisfies:

$$i^2 = -1.$$

Every _____ can be written in the form a + bi, where a and b are real numbers called the real part and the imaginary part of the _____, respectively.

Complex numbers are a field, and thus have addition, subtraction, multiplication, and division operations. These operations extend the corresponding operations on real numbers, although with a number of additional elegant and useful properties, e.g., negative real numbers can be obtained by squaring complex (imaginary) numbers.

 a. -module
 b. -equivalence
 c. 2-bridge knot
 d. Complex number

36. In mathematics and, in particular, functional analysis, _____ is a mathematical operation on two functions f and g, producing a third function that is typically viewed as a modified version of one of the original functions. _____ is similar to cross-correlation. It has applications that include statistics, computer vision, image and signal processing, electrical engineering, and differential equations.
 a. 2-bridge knot
 b. -module
 c. -equivalence
 d. Convolution

37. In mathematics, an _____ is a complex number whose squared value is a real number less than or equal to zero. The imaginary unit, denoted by i or j, is an example of an _____. If y is a real number, then i·y is an _____, because:

$$(i \cdot y)^2 = i^2 \cdot y^2 = -y^2 \leq 0.$$

Imaginary numbers were defined in 1572 by Rafael Bombelli.

 a. AKS primality test
 b. Abelian P-root group
 c. Imaginary number
 d. ADE classification

38. In mathematics, a _____ of a number x is any number which, when repeatedly multiplied by itself, eventually yields x:

$$r \times r \times \cdots \times r = x.$$

In terms of exponentiation, r is a _____ of x if

$$r^n = x$$

for some positive integer n. For example, 2 is a _____ of 16 since $2^4 = 2 \times 2 \times 2 \times 2 = 16$.

The number n is called the degree of the _____.

    a. Cubic function
    b. Difference of two squares
    c. Rationalisation
    d. Root

39. In mathematics, a _____ is a circle with a unit radius, i.e., a circle whose radius is 1. Frequently, especially in trigonometry, 'the' _____ is the circle of radius 1 centered at the origin (0, 0) in the Cartesian coordinate system in the Euclidean plane. The _____ is often denoted S^1; the generalization to higher dimensions is the unit sphere.
    a. ADE classification
    b. Abelian P-root group
    c. AKS primality test
    d. Unit circle

40. In mathematics, a _____ is a flat surface. Planes can arise as subspaces of some higher dimensional space, as with the walls of a room, or they may enjoy an independent existence in their own right, as in the setting of Euclidean geometry
    a. -equivalence
    b. -module
    c. Similarity
    d. Plane

41. In mathematics, the _____ of two sets A and B is the set that contains all elements of A that also belong to B (or equivalently, all elements of B that also belong to A), but no other elements.

Chapter 3. ORTHOGONALITY

For explanation of the symbols used in this article, refer to the table of mathematical symbols.

The _____ of A and B

The _____ of A and B is written 'A ∩ B'.

   a. AKS primality test
   b. Abelian P-root group
   c. ADE classification
   d. Intersection

42. In mathematics, the _____ of a vector space V is the cardinality (i.e. the number of vectors) of a basis of V. It is sometimes called Hamel _____ or algebraic _____ to distinguish it from other types of _____. All bases of a vector space have equal cardinality and so the _____ of a vector space is uniquely defined. The _____ of the vector space V over the field F can be written as $\dim_F(V)$ or as $[V : F]$, read '_____ of V over F'.

   a. Partial trace
   b. Cofactor
   c. Dual basis
   d. Dimension

43. In abstract algebra, an _____ is a bijective map f such that both f and its inverse f^{-1} are homomorphisms, i.e., structure-preserving mappings. In the more general setting of category theory, an _____ is a morphism $f:X \to Y$ in a category for which there exists an 'inverse' $f^{-1}:Y \to X$, with the property that both $f^{-1}f=id_X$ and $ff^{-1}=id_Y$.

Informally, an _____ is a kind of mapping between objects, which shows a relationship between two properties or operations.

   a. ADE classification
   b. Endomorphism
   c. Epimorphism
   d. Isomorphism

44. The column _____ of a matrix A is the maximal number of linearly independent columns of A. Likewise, the row _____ is the maximal number of linearly independent rows of A.

Since the column _____ and the row _____ are always equal, they are simply called the _____ of A. More abstractly, it is the dimension of the image of A. For the proofs, see, e.g., Murase (1960), Andrea ' Wong (1960), Williams ' Cater (1968), Mackiw (1995).) It is commonly denoted by either rk(A) or _____ A.

- a. Schur complement
- b. Rank
- c. Split-complex number
- d. Generalized Pauli matrices

45. In mathematics, a _____ is a matrix formed by selecting certain rows and columns from a bigger matrix. That is, as an array, it is cut down to those entries constrained by row and column.

For example

$$\mathbf{A} = \begin{bmatrix} a_{11} & a_{12} & a_{13} & a_{14} \\ a_{21} & a_{22} & a_{23} & a_{24} \\ a_{31} & a_{32} & a_{33} & a_{34} \end{bmatrix}.$$

Then

$$\mathbf{A}[1,2;1,3,4] = \begin{bmatrix} a_{11} & a_{13} & a_{14} \\ a_{21} & a_{23} & a_{24} \end{bmatrix}$$

is a _____ of A formed by rows 1,2 and columns 1,3,4.

- a. Submatrix
- b. Quasideterminant
- c. Smith normal form
- d. Lie product formula

46. In probability theory and statistics, _____ is a measure of how much two variables change together (variance is a special case of the _____ when the two variables are identical.)

If two variables tend to vary together (that is, when one of them is above its expected value, then the other variable tends to be above its expected value too), then the _____ between the two variables will be positive. On the other hand, if one of them tends to be above its expected value when the other variable is below its expected value, then the _____ between the two variables will be negative.

a. -equivalence
b. -module
c. 2-bridge knot
d. Covariance

47. In statistics and probability theory, the _____ or dispersion matrix is a matrix of covariances between elements of a random vector. It is the natural generalization to higher dimensions of the concept of the variance of a scalar-valued random variable.

If entries in the column vector

$$X = \begin{bmatrix} X_1 \\ \vdots \\ X_n \end{bmatrix}$$

are random variables, each with finite variance, then the _____ Σ is the matrix whose (i, j) entry is the covariance

$$\Sigma_{ij} = \text{cov}(X_i, X_j) = \text{E}\big[(X_i - \mu_i)(X_j - \mu_j)\big]$$

where

$$\mu_i = \text{E}(X_i)$$

is the expected value of the ith entry in the vector X. In other words, we have

$$\Sigma = \begin{bmatrix} \text{E}[(X_1 - \mu_1)(X_1 - \mu_1)] & \text{E}[(X_1 - \mu_1)(X_2 - \mu_2)] & \cdots & \text{E}[(X_1 - \mu_1)(X_n - \mu_n)] \\ \text{E}[(X_2 - \mu_2)(X_1 - \mu_1)] & \text{E}[(X_2 - \mu_2)(X_2 - \mu_2)] & \cdots & \text{E}[(X_2 - \mu_2)(X_n - \mu_n)] \\ \vdots & \vdots & \ddots & \vdots \\ \text{E}[(X_n - \mu_n)(X_1 - \mu_1)] & \text{E}[(X_n - \mu_n)(X_2 - \mu_2)] & \cdots & \text{E}[(X_n - \mu_n)(X_n - \mu_n)] \end{bmatrix}.$$

The inverse of this matrix, Σ^{-1}, is called the inverse _____, concentration matrix or precision matrix.

a. Covariance matrix
b. -equivalence
c. 2-bridge knot
d. -module

48. In abstract algebra, the _____ is a construction which combines several modules into a new, larger module. The result of the direct summation of modules is the 'smallest general' module which contains the given modules as subspaces. This is an example of a coproduct.
   a. Direct sum
   b. Frame
   c. Finite dimensional von Neumann algebra
   d. Schmidt decomposition

49. In mathematics and group theory, a _____ system for the action of a group G on a set X is a partition of X that is G-invariant. In terms of the associated equivalence relation on X, G-invariance means that

$x \equiv y$ implies $gx \equiv gy$

for all g in G and all x, y in X. The action of G on X determines a natural action of G on any _____ system for X.

Each element of the _____ system is called a _____.

   a. Symmetric group
   b. Frobenius group
   c. Parker vector
   d. Block

Chapter 4. DETERMINANTS

1. In vector calculus, the _____ is shorthand for either the _____ matrix or its determinant, the _____ determinant.

In algebraic geometry the _____ of a curve means the _____ variety: a group variety associated to the curve, in which the curve can be embedded.

These concepts are all named after the mathematician Carl Gustav Jacob Jacobi.

   a. Laplace operator
   b. Hessian matrix
   c. Critical point
   d. Jacobian

2. In algebra, a _____ is a function depending on n that associates a scalar, det(A), to an n×n square matrix A. The fundamental geometric meaning of a _____ is a scale factor for measure when A is regarded as a linear transformation. Determinants are important both in calculus, where they enter the substitution rule for several variables, and in multilinear algebra.

For a fixed nonnegative integer n, there is a unique _____ function for the n×n matrices over any commutative ring R. In particular, this function exists when R is the field of real or complex numbers.

   a. Leibniz formula
   b. Functional determinant
   c. Pfaffian
   d. Determinant

3. _____, developed in 1854 by George Boole in his book An Investigation of the Laws of Thought, is a variant of ordinary algebra as taught in high school. _____ differs from ordinary algebra in three ways: in the values that variables may assume, which are of a logical instead of a numeric character, prototypically 0 and 1; in the operations applicable to those values; and in the properties of those operations, that is, the laws they obey.

Whereas high school algebra deals mainly with real numbers, _____ deals with the values 0 and 1.

   a. Boolean logic
   b. Free Boolean algebra
   c. Reed-Muller expansion
   d. Boolean algebra

4. In several fields of mathematics the term _____ is used with different but closely related meanings. They all relate to the notion of mapping the elements of a set to other elements of the same set, i.e., exchanging (or 'permuting') elements of a set.

The general concept of _____ can be defined more formally in different contexts:

In combinatorics, a _____ is usually understood to be a sequence containing each element from a finite set once, and only once.

- a. Binary function
- b. Rupture field
- c. Permutation
- d. Near-field

5. In mathematics, in matrix theory, a _____ is a square (0,1)-matrix that has exactly one entry 1 in each row and each column and 0's elsewhere. Each such matrix represents a specific permutation of m elements and, when used to multiply another matrix, can produce that permutation in the rows or columns of the other matrix.

Given a permutation π of m elements,

$$\pi : \{1, \ldots, m\} \to \{1, \ldots, m\}$$

given in two-line form by

$$\begin{pmatrix} 1 & 2 & \cdots & m \\ \pi(1) & \pi(2) & \cdots & \pi(m) \end{pmatrix},$$

its _____ is the m × m matrix P_π whose entries are all 0 except that in row i, the entry π(i) equals 1.

- a. Skew-symmetric
- b. Permutation matrix
- c. Main diagonal
- d. Hessenberg matrix

6. In mathematics, a _____ is a rectangular array of numbers. This way, matrices can record data that depend on multiple parameters. In particular they are used to keep track of the coefficients of multiple linear equations. Matrices are closely connected to linear transformations, which are higher-dimensional analogs of linear functions, i.e., functions of the form f(x) = c Â· x, where c is a constant. This map corresponds to a _____ with one row and column, with entry c. In addition to a number of elementary, entrywise operations such as _____ addition a key notion is _____ multiplication, which displays a number of features not encountered in numbers; for example, products of matrices depend on the order of the factors, unlike products of real numbers, say, where c Â· d = d Â· c for any two numbers c and d.

a. Commutativity
b. Polynomial expression
c. Matrix
d. Heap

7. In the mathematical discipline of linear algebra, a _____ is a special kind of square matrix where the entries either below or above the main diagonal are zero. Because matrix equations with triangular matrices are easier to solve they are very important in numerical analysis. The LU decomposition gives an algorithm to decompose any invertible matrix A into a normed lower triangle matrix L and an upper triangle matrix U.
   a. Hilbert matrix
   b. Circulant matrix
   c. Diagonally dominant
   d. Triangular matrix

8. In linear algebra, the _____ describes a particular construction that is useful for calculating both the determinant and inverse of square matrices. Specifically the _____ of the (i, j) entry of a matrix, also known as the (i, j) _____ of that matrix, is the signed minor of that entry.

Finding the minors of a matrix A is a multi-step process:

1. Choose an entry a_{ij} from the matrix.
2. Cross out the entries that lie in the corresponding row i and column j.
3. Rewrite the matrix without the marked entries.
4. Obtain the determinant M_{ij} of this new matrix.

M_{ij} is termed the minor for entry a_{ij}.

If i + j is an even number, the _____ C_{ij} of a_{ij} coincides with its minor:

$$C_{ij} = M_{ij}.$$

Otherwise, it is equal to the additive inverse of its minor:

$$C_{ij} = -M_{ij}.$$

If A is a square matrix, then the minor of its entry a_{ij}, also known as the i,j or (i,j), or (i,j)th minor of A, is denoted by M_{ij} and is defined to be the determinant of the submatrix obtained by removing from A its i-th row and j-th column.

a. Cofactor
b. Complex structure
c. Coefficient matrix
d. Resolvent set

9. In linear algebra, a _____ of a matrix A is the determinant of some smaller square matrix, cut down from A by removing one or more of its rows or columns. Minors obtained by removing just one row and one column from square matrices (first minors) are required for calculating matrix cofactors, which in turn are useful for computing both the determinant and inverse of square matrices.

a. Minor
b. Rng
c. Purification
d. Supergroup

10. In mathematics and group theory, a _____ system for the action of a group G on a set X is a partition of X that is G-invariant. In terms of the associated equivalence relation on X, G-invariance means that

x ≡ y implies gx ≡ gy

for all g in G and all x, y in X. The action of G on X determines a natural action of G on any _____ system for X.

Each element of the _____ system is called a _____.

a. Frobenius group
b. Symmetric group
c. Parker vector
d. Block

11. In mathematics, a _____ is a matrix formed by selecting certain rows and columns from a bigger matrix. That is, as an array, it is cut down to those entries constrained by row and column.

For example

$$\mathbf{A} = \begin{bmatrix} a_{11} & a_{12} & a_{13} & a_{14} \\ a_{21} & a_{22} & a_{23} & a_{24} \\ a_{31} & a_{32} & a_{33} & a_{34} \end{bmatrix}.$$

Then

$$\mathbf{A}[1,2;1,3,4] = \begin{bmatrix} a_{11} & a_{13} & a_{14} \\ a_{21} & a_{23} & a_{24} \end{bmatrix}$$

is a _____ of A formed by rows 1,2 and columns 1,3,4.

   a. Quasideterminant
   b. Smith normal form
   c. Lie product formula
   d. Submatrix

12. In linear algebra, the _____ or classical adjoint of a square matrix is a matrix which plays a role similar to the inverse of a matrix; it can however be defined for any square matrix without the need to perform any divisions.

The _____ has sometimes been called the 'adjoint', but that terminology is ambiguous. Today, 'adjoint' of a matrix normally refers to its corresponding adjoint operator, which is its conjugate transpose.

   a. Adjugate
   b. ADE classification
   c. Abelian P-root group
   d. AKS primality test

13. In linear algebra, _____ is an efficient algorithm for solving systems of linear equations, finding the rank of a matrix, and calculating the inverse of an invertible square matrix. _____ is named after German mathematician and scientist Carl Friedrich Gauss.

Elementary row operations are used to reduce a matrix to row echelon form.

   a. -equivalence
   b. -module
   c. 2-bridge knot
   d. Gaussian elimination

14. In linear algebra and the theory of matrices, the _____ of a matrix block (i.e., a submatrix within a larger matrix) is defined as follows. Suppose A, B, C, D are respectively p×p, p×q, q×p and q×q matrices, and D is invertible. Let

$$M = \begin{bmatrix} A & B \\ C & D \end{bmatrix}$$

so that M is a (p+q)×(p+q) matrix.

   a. Fundamental theorem of linear algebra
   b. Homogeneous function
   c. Projection-valued measure
   d. Schur complement

15. In discrete mathematics and predominantly in set theory, a _____ is a concept used in comparisons of sets to refer to the unique values of one set in relation to another. The terms 'absolute' and 'relative' _____ refer to more specific applications of the concept, with universal complements referring to elements unique to the universal set and the latter referring to the unique elements of one set in relation to another. In this image, the universal set is represented by the border of the image, and the set A as a disc.

   a. -equivalence
   b. -module
   c. Complement
   d. Pointed set

16. In algebraic topology, a simplicial k-_____ is a formal linear combination of k-simplices.

Integration is defined on chains by taking the linear combination of integrals over the simplices in the _____ with coefficients typically integers. The set of all k-chains forms a group and the sequence of these groups is called a _____ complex.

   a. Tesseract
   b. Bockstein homomorphism
   c. Combinatorial topology
   d. Chain

Chapter 5. EIGENVALUES AND EIGENVECTORS

1. For each eigenvector of a linear transformation, there is a corresponding scalar value called an _____ for that vector, which determines the amount the eigenvector is scaled under the linear transformation. For example, an _____ of +2 means that the eigenvector is doubled in length and points in the same direction. An _____ of +1 means that the eigenvector is unchanged, while an _____ of −1 means that the eigenvector is reversed in sense.
   a. Abelian P-root group
   b. ADE classification
   c. AKS primality test
   d. Eigenvalue

2. For each _____ of a linear transformation, there is a corresponding scalar value called an eigenvalue for that vector, which determines the amount the _____ is scaled under the linear transformation. For example, an eigenvalue of +2 means that the _____ is doubled in length and points in the same direction. An eigenvalue of +1 means that the _____ is unchanged, while an eigenvalue of −1 means that the _____ is reversed in sense.
   a. Eigenvector
   b. Abelian P-root group
   c. ADE classification
   d. AKS primality test

3. In mathematics, the _____ of a ring R, often denoted char(R), is defined to be the smallest number of times one must add the ring's multiplicative identity element (1) to itself to get the additive identity element (0); the ring is said to have _____ zero if this repeated sum never reaches the additive identity. That is, char(R) is the smallest positive number n such that

$$\underbrace{1 + \cdots + 1}_{n \text{ summands}} = 0$$

if such a number n exists, and 0 otherwise. The _____ may also be taken to be the exponent of the ring's additive group, that is, the smallest positive n such that

$$\underbrace{a + \cdots + a}_{n \text{ summands}} = 0$$

for every element a of the ring (again, if n exists; otherwise zero.)

   a. Free ideal ring
   b. Hereditary
   c. Coherent ring
   d. Characteristic

Chapter 5. EIGENVALUES AND EIGENVECTORS

4. In discrete mathematics, the _____ is used when solving recurrence problems. One can specify a recurrence relation of the form

$$t_n = At_{n-1} + Bt_{n-2}$$

where the value of t_n is dependent on the values of t_{n-1} and t_{n-2}. When solving a recurrence relation, the goal is to eliminate this dependency and derive an equation of the form

$$t_n = c_1 r_1^n + c_2 r_2^n,$$

where c_1 and c_2 are constants and r_1 and r_2 are the roots of the _____

$$r^2 - Ar - B = 0,$$

where A and B are the constants defined in the original recurrence relation.

   a. -equivalence
   b. -module
   c. 2-bridge knot
   d. Characteristic equation

5. In linear algebra, one associates a polynomial to every square matrix, its _____. This polynomial encodes several important properties of the matrix, most notably its eigenvalues, its determinant and its trace.

Given a square matrix A, we want to find a polynomial whose roots are precisely the eigenvalues of A. For a diagonal matrix A, the _____ is easy to define: if the diagonal entries are a_1, a_2, a_3, etc.

   a. Constant term
   b. Characteristic polynomial
   c. Quasi-polynomial
   d. Square-free polynomial

6. In linear algebra and functional analysis, a _____ is a linear transformation P from a vector space to itself such that $P^2 = P$. It leaves its image unchanged. Though abstract, this definition of '_____' formalizes and generalizes the idea of graphical _____.

a. Convolution power
b. C_0-semigroup
c. Lumer-Phillips theorem
d. Projection

7. In linear algebra, the _____ of an n-by-n square matrix A is defined to be the sum of the elements on the main diagonal (the diagonal from the upper left to the lower right) of A, i.e.,

$$\text{tr}(A) = a_{11} + a_{22} + \cdots + a_{nn} = \sum_{i=1}^{n} a_{ii}$$

where a_{ij} represents the entry on the ith row and jth column of A. Equivalently, the _____ of a matrix is the sum of its eigenvalues, making it an invariant with respect to a change of basis. This characterization can be used to define the _____ for a linear operator in general.

Note that the _____ is only defined for a square matrix (i.e. n×n.)

a. Trace
b. Dot product
c. Defective matrix
d. Coefficient matrix

8. In linear algebra, the _____ of the monic polynomial

$$p(t) = c_0 + c_1 t + \ldots + c_{n-1} t^{n-1} + t^n$$

is the square matrix defined as

$$C(p) = \begin{bmatrix} 0 & 0 & \ldots & 0 & -c_0 \\ 1 & 0 & \ldots & 0 & -c_1 \\ 0 & 1 & \ldots & 0 & -c_2 \\ \vdots & \vdots & \vdots & \vdots & \vdots \\ 0 & 0 & \ldots & 1 & -c_{n-1} \end{bmatrix}.$$

With this convention, and writing the basis as $v_1, \ldots, v_n$, one has $Cv_i = C^{i-1}v_1 = v_{i+1}$ (for i < n), and v_1 generates V as a K[C]-module: C cycles basis vectors.

Chapter 5. EIGENVALUES AND EIGENVECTORS

Some authors use the transpose of this matrix, which (dually) cycles coordinates, and is more convenient for some purposes, like linear recursive relations.

The characteristic polynomial as well as the minimal polynomial of C(p) are equal to p; in this sense, the matrix C(p) is the 'companion' of the polynomial p.

a. Levinson recursion
b. Matrix representation
c. Wilkinson matrices
d. Companion matrix

9. In mathematics, a _____ is a rectangular array of numbers. This way, matrices can record data that depend on multiple parameters. In particular they are used to keep track of the coefficients of multiple linear equations. Matrices are closely connected to linear transformations, which are higher-dimensional analogs of linear functions, i.e., functions of the form f(x) = c Â· x, where c is a constant. This map corresponds to a _____ with one row and column, with entry c. In addition to a number of elementary, entrywise operations such as _____ addition a key notion is _____ multiplication, which displays a number of features not encountered in numbers; for example, products of matrices depend on the order of the factors, unlike products of real numbers, say, where c Â· d = d Â· c for any two numbers c and d.

a. Matrix
b. Heap
c. Commutativity
d. Polynomial expression

10. In linear algebra, a family of vectors is _____ if none of them can be written as a linear combination of finitely many other vectors in the collection. A family of vectors which is not _____ is called linearly dependent. For instance, in the three-dimensional real vector space $\mathbb{R}^3$ we have the following example.

a. Composition ring
b. Grothendieck group
c. Derivative algebra
d. Linearly independent

11. In mathematics, the complex numbers are an extension of the real numbers obtained by adjoining an imaginary unit, denoted i, which satisfies:

$$i^2 = -1.$$

Every _____ can be written in the form a + bi, where a and b are real numbers called the real part and the imaginary part of the _____, respectively.

Chapter 5. EIGENVALUES AND EIGENVECTORS

Complex numbers are a field, and thus have addition, subtraction, multiplication, and division operations. These operations extend the corresponding operations on real numbers, although with a number of additional elegant and useful properties, e.g., negative real numbers can be obtained by squaring complex (imaginary) numbers.

  a. -equivalence
  b. 2-bridge knot
  c. -module
  d. Complex number

12. In mathematics, an _____ is a complex number whose squared value is a real number less than or equal to zero. The imaginary unit, denoted by i or j, is an example of an _____. If y is a real number, then i·y is an _____, because:

$$(i \cdot y)^2 = i^2 \cdot y^2 = -y^2 \leq 0.$$

Imaginary numbers were defined in 1572 by Rafael Bombelli.

  a. AKS primality test
  b. ADE classification
  c. Abelian P-root group
  d. Imaginary number

13. In geometry and linear algebra, a _____ is a transformation in a plane or in space that describes the motion of a rigid body around a fixed point. A _____ is different from a translation, which has no fixed points, and from a reflection, which 'flips' the bodies it is transforming. A _____ and the above-mentioned transformations are isometries; they leave the distance between any two points unchanged after the transformation.

  a. Rotation
  b. Reflection
  c. Real matrices
  d. Shear mappings

14. In mathematics, the Cauchy-_____ the Cauchy inequality is a useful inequality encountered in many different settings, such as linear algebra applied to vectors, in analysis applied to infinite series and integration of products, and in probability theory, applied to variances and covariances. The general formulation of the Heisenberg uncertainty principle is derived using the Cauchy-_____ in the Hilbert space of pure quantum states.

The inequality for sums was published by , while the corresponding inequality for integrals was first stated by and rediscovered by

Chapter 5. EIGENVALUES AND EIGENVECTORS

a. Schwarz inequality
b. -equivalence
c. 2-bridge knot
d. -module

15. In mathematics, an _____ is a statement about the relative size or order of two objects, or about whether they are the same or not

- The notation a < b means that a is less than b.
- The notation a > b means that a is greater than b.
- The notation a ≠ b means that a is not equal to b, but does not say that one is bigger than the other or even that they can be compared in size.

In all these cases, a is not equal to b, hence, '_____'.

These relations are known as strict _____

- The notation a ≤ b means that a is less than or equal to b (or, equivalently, not greater than b);
- The notation a ≥ b means that a is greater than or equal to b (or, equivalently, not smaller than b);

An additional use of the notation is to show that one quantity is much greater than another, normally by several orders of magnitude.

- The notation a ≪ b means that a is much less than b.
- The notation a ≫ b means that a is much greater than b.

If the sense of the _____ is the same for all values of the variables for which its members are defined, then the _____ is called an 'absolute' or 'unconditional' _____. If the sense of an _____ holds only for certain values of the variables involved, but is reversed or destroyed for other values of the variables, it is called a conditional _____.

One can apply the same algebraic operations to inequalities as one would apply for solving equalities. For example, to find x for the _____ 10x > 20 one would divide 20 by 10 to obtain x > 2.

a. Inequality
b. AKS primality test
c. Abelian P-root group
d. ADE classification

16. In mathematics, a _____ of a number x is a number r such that $r^2 = x$, or, in other words, a number r whose square (the result of multiplying the number by itself) is x.

Chapter 5. EIGENVALUES AND EIGENVECTORS

Every non-negative real number x has a unique non-negative _____, called the principal _____, which is denoted with a radical symbol as $\sqrt{x}$, or, using exponent notation, as $x^{1/2}$. For example, the principal _____ of 9 is 3, denoted $\sqrt{9} = 3$, because $3^2 = 3 \times 3 = 9$.

 a. 2-bridge knot
 b. -module
 c. -equivalence
 d. Square root

17. In mathematics, a _____ of a number x is any number which, when repeatedly multiplied by itself, eventually yields x:

$$r \times r \times \cdots \times r = x.$$

In terms of exponentiation, r is a _____ of x if

$$r^n = x$$

for some positive integer n. For example, 2 is a _____ of 16 since $2^4 = 2 \times 2 \times 2 \times 2 = 16$.

The number n is called the degree of the _____.

 a. Cubic function
 b. Difference of two squares
 c. Root
 d. Rationalisation

18. Economics is the social science that studies the production, distribution, and consumption of goods and services. The term economics comes from the Ancient Greek oá¼°κονομῖα from oá¼¶κος (oikos, 'house') + νÏŒμος (nomos, 'custom' or 'law'), hence 'rules of the house(hold)'. Current _____ models developed out of the broader field of political economy in the late 19th century, owing to a desire to use an empirical approach more akin to the physical sciences.
 a. AKS primality test
 b. ADE classification
 c. Abelian P-root group
 d. Economic

19. A _____ is a matrix in which all the elements are greater than zero. The set of positive matrices is a subset of all non-negative matrices.

Chapter 5. EIGENVALUES AND EIGENVECTORS

A non-negative matrix can represent a transition matrix for a Markov chain.

   a. Positive matrix
   b. -equivalence
   c. -module
   d. 2-bridge knot

20. In linear algebra, a _____ of a matrix A is a nonzero vector v, which has associated with it an eigenvalue λ having algebraic multiplicity k ≥1, satisfying

$$(A - \lambda I)^k \mathbf{v} = 0.$$

Ordinary eigenvectors are obtained for k=1.

Generalized eigenvectors are needed to form a complete basis of a defective matrix, which is a matrix in which there are fewer linearly independent eigenvectors than eigenvalues. The generalized eigenvectors do form a complete basis, as follows from the Jordan form of a matrix.

   a. Generalized eigenvector
   b. Vectorization
   c. Schmidt decomposition
   d. Jordan normal form

21. In mathematics, two vectors are _____ if they are perpendicular, i.e., they form a right angle. The word comes from the Greek á½€ρθÏŒς , meaning 'straight', and γωνῖα (gonia), meaning 'angle'. For example, a subway and the street above, although they do not physically intersect, are _____ if they cross at a right angle.
   a. Unital
   b. Expression
   c. Embedding
   d. Orthogonal

22. In linear algebra, an _____ is a square matrix with real entries whose columns (or rows) are orthogonal unit vectors (i.e., orthonormal.) Equivalently, a matrix Q is orthogonal if its transpose is equal to its inverse:

$$Q^T Q = Q Q^T = I.$$

Chapter 5. EIGENVALUES AND EIGENVECTORS

As a linear transformation, an _____ preserves the dot product of vectors, and therefore acts as an isometry of Euclidean space, such as a rotation or reflection.

The set of n × n orthogonal matrices forms a group O(n), known as the orthogonal group.

- a. Unistochastic matrix
- b. Alternating sign matrix
- c. Unimodular matrix
- d. Orthogonal matrix

23. In abstract algebra, the _____ of a module is a measure of the module's 'size'. It is defined as the _____ of the longest ascending chain of submodules and is a generalization of the concept of dimension for vector spaces. The modules with finite _____ share many important properties with finite-dimensional vector spaces.
- a. Morita equivalence
- b. Supermodule
- c. Finitely generated module
- d. Length

24. In mathematics, the _____ of a real number is its numerical value without regard to its sign. So, for example, 3 is the _____ of both 3 and −3.

The _____ of a number a is denoted by $|a|$.

- a. AKS primality test
- b. ADE classification
- c. Absolute value
- d. Abelian P-root group

25. In mathematics, the (formal) _____ of a complex vector space V is the complex vector space $\overline{V}$ consisting of all formal complex conjugates of elements of V. That is, $\overline{V}$ is a vector space whose elements are in one-to-one correspondence with the elements of V:

$$\overline{V} = \{\overline{v} \mid v \in V\},$$

Chapter 5. EIGENVALUES AND EIGENVECTORS

with the following rules for addition and scalar multiplication:

$$\overline{v} + \overline{w} = \overline{v+w} \quad \text{and} \quad \alpha \overline{v} = \overline{\overline{\alpha} v}.$$

Here v and w are vectors in V, α is a complex number, and $\overline{\alpha}$ denotes the _____ of α.

In the case where V is a linear subspace of $\mathbb{C}^n$, the formal _____ $\overline{V}$ is naturally isomorphic to the actual _____ subspace of V in $\mathbb{C}^n$.

- a. Complex conjugate
- b. Conjugate transpose
- c. Binomial inverse theorem
- d. Polynomial basis

26. In algebra, a _____ of an element in a quadratic extension field of a field K is its image under the unique non-identity automorphism of the extended field that fixes K. If the extension is generated by a square root of an element r of K, then the _____ of $a + b\sqrt{r}$ is $a - b\sqrt{r}$ for $a, b \in K$, and in particular in the case of the field C of complex numbers as an extension of the field R of real numbers (where r = − 1), the complex _____ of a + bi is a − bi.

Forming the sum or product of any element of the extension field with its _____ always gives an element of K. This can be used to rewrite a quotient of numbers in the extended field so that the denominator lies in K, by multiplying numerator and denominator by the _____ of the denominator. This process is called rationalization of the denominator, in particular if K is the field Q of rational numbers.

- a. K-theory
- b. Digital root
- c. Field arithmetic
- d. Conjugate

27. In mathematics, in the field of algebraic number theory, a _____ is a formal product of places of an algebraic number field. It is used to encode ramification data for abelian extensions of number field.

Let K be an algebraic number field with ring of integers R. A _____ is a formal product

$$\mathbf{m} = \prod_{\mathbf{p}} \mathbf{p}^{\nu(\mathbf{p})}$$

where p runs over all places of K, finite or infinite, the exponents v are zero except for finitely many p, for real places r we have v(r)=0 or 1 and for complex places v=0.

Chapter 5. EIGENVALUES AND EIGENVECTORS

a. Different ideal
b. Modulus
c. Quadratic field
d. Principal ideal theorem

28. In mathematics, a _____ is a flat surface. Planes can arise as subspaces of some higher dimensional space, as with the walls of a room, or they may enjoy an independent existence in their own right, as in the setting of Euclidean geometry
a. Plane
b. Similarity
c. -module
d. -equivalence

29. In mathematics, a _____ in a (unital) ring R is an invertible element of R, i.e. an element u such that there is a v in R with

uv = vu = 1_R, where 1_R is the multiplicative identity element.

That is, u is an invertible element of the multiplicative monoid of R. If $0 \neq 1$ in the ring, then 0 is not a _____.

Unfortunately, the term _____ is also used to refer to the identity element 1_R of the ring, in expressions like ring with a _____ or _____ ring, and also e.g. '_____' matrix.

a. Ore extension
b. Ascending chain condition on principal ideals
c. Ore condition
d. Unit

30. In mathematics, a _____ is a circle with a unit radius, i.e., a circle whose radius is 1. Frequently, especially in trigonometry, 'the' _____ is the circle of radius 1 centered at the origin (0, 0) in the Cartesian coordinate system in the Euclidean plane. The _____ is often denoted S^1; the generalization to higher dimensions is the unit sphere.
a. AKS primality test
b. Abelian P-root group
c. ADE classification
d. Unit circle

Chapter 5. EIGENVALUES AND EIGENVECTORS

31. In mathematics, the _____, Hermitian transpose, or adjoint matrix of an m-by-n matrix A with complex entries is the n-by-m matrix A* obtained from A by taking the transpose and then taking the complex conjugate of each entry. The _____ is formally defined by

$$(A^*)_{ij} = \overline{A_{ji}}$$

where the subscripts denote the i,j-th entry, for $1 \leq i \leq n$ and $1 \leq j \leq m$, and the overbar denotes a scalar complex conjugate. (The complex conjugate of a + bi, where a and b are reals, is a − bi.)

a. Dual spaces
b. Change of basis
c. Conjugate transpose
d. Complex conjugate

32. In linear algebra, the _____ of a matrix A is another matrix A^T (also written A′, A^{tr} or ^tA) created by any one of the following equivalent actions:

- write the rows of A as the columns of A^T
- write the columns of A as the rows of A^T
- reflect A by its main diagonal (which starts from the top left) to obtain A^T

Formally, the _____ of an m × n matrix A with elements A_{ij} is the n × m matrix

$$A^T_{ij} = A_{ji} \text{ for } 1 \leq i \leq n, 1 \leq j \leq m.$$

The _____ of a scalar is the same scalar.

- $\begin{bmatrix} 1 & 2 \end{bmatrix}^T = \begin{bmatrix} 1 \\ 2 \end{bmatrix}.$

- $\begin{bmatrix} 1 & 2 \\ 3 & 4 \end{bmatrix}^T = \begin{bmatrix} 1 & 3 \\ 2 & 4 \end{bmatrix}.$

- $\begin{bmatrix} 1 & 2 \\ 3 & 4 \\ 5 & 6 \end{bmatrix}^T = \begin{bmatrix} 1 & 3 & 5 \\ 2 & 4 & 6 \end{bmatrix}.$

Chapter 5. EIGENVALUES AND EIGENVECTORS

For matrices A, B and scalar c we have the following properties of _____:

1. $\left(\mathbf{A}^{T}\right)^{T} = \mathbf{A}$

    Taking the _____ is an involution (self inverse.)

- $(\mathbf{A} + \mathbf{B})^{T} = \mathbf{A}^{T} + \mathbf{B}^{T}$

    The _____ respects addition.

- $(\mathbf{AB})^{T} = \mathbf{B}^{T}\mathbf{A}^{T}$

    Note that the order of the factors reverses. From this one can deduce that a square matrix A is invertible if and only if A^T is invertible, and in this case we have $(A^{-1})^T = (A^T)^{-1}$. It is relatively easy to extend this result to the general case of multiple matrices, where we find that $(ABC...XYZ)^T = Z^TY^TX^T...C^TB^TA^T$.

- $(c\mathbf{A})^{T} = c\mathbf{A}^{T}$

    The _____ of a scalar is the same scalar. Together with (2), this states that the _____ is a linear map from the space of m × n matrices to the space of all n × m matrices.

- $\det(\mathbf{A}^{T}) = \det(\mathbf{A})$

    The determinant of a square matrix is the same as that of its _____.

- The dot product of two column vectors a and b can be computed as

    $$\mathbf{a} \cdot \mathbf{b} = \mathbf{a}^{T}\mathbf{b},$$

    which is written as $a_i b^i$ in Einstein notation.
- If A has only real entries, then A^TA is a positive-semidefinite matrix.
- $\left(\mathbf{A}^{T}\right)^{-1} = \left(\mathbf{A}^{-1}\right)^{T}$

    The _____ of an invertible matrix is also invertible, and its inverse is the _____ of the inverse of the original matrix.

- If A is a square matrix, then its eigenvalues are equal to the eigenvalues of its _____.

A square matrix whose _____ is equal to itself is called a symmetric matrix; that is, A is symmetric if

$$\mathbf{A}^T = \mathbf{A}.$$

A square matrix whose _____ is also its inverse is called an orthogonal matrix; that is, G is orthogonal if

$$\mathbf{G}\mathbf{G}^T = \mathbf{G}^T\mathbf{G} = \mathbf{I}_n,$$ the identity matrix, i.e. $G^T = G^{-1}$.

A square matrix whose _____ is equal to its negative is called skew-symmetric matrix; that is, A is skew-symmetric if

$$\mathbf{A}^T = -\mathbf{A}.$$

The conjugate _____ of the complex matrix A, written as A^*, is obtained by taking the _____ of A and the complex conjugate of each entry:

$$\mathbf{A}^* = (\overline{\mathbf{A}})^T = \overline{(\mathbf{A}^T)}.$$

If f: V→W is a linear map between vector spaces V and W with nondegenerate bilinear forms, we define the _____ of f to be the linear map ^tf : W→V, determined by

$$B_V(v, {}^tf(w)) = B_W(f(v), w) \quad \forall\, v \in V, w \in W.$$

Here, B_V and B_W are the bilinear forms on V and W respectively. The matrix of the _____ of a map is the transposed matrix only if the bases are orthonormal with respect to their bilinear forms.

Over a complex vector space, one often works with sesquilinear forms instead of bilinear (conjugate-linear in one argument.)

   a. Drazin inverse
   b. Tridiagonal matrix
   c. Levinson recursion
   d. Transpose

33. A _____ is a square matrix with complex entries which is equal to its own conjugate transpose -- that is, the element in the ith row and jth column is equal to the complex conjugate of the element in the jth row and ith column, for all indices i and j:

Chapter 5. EIGENVALUES AND EIGENVECTORS

$$a_{i,j} = \overline{a_{j,i}}.$$

If the conjugate transpose of a matrix A is denoted by $A^\dagger$, then the Hermitian property can be written concisely as

$$A = A^\dagger.$$

For example,

$$\begin{bmatrix} 3 & 2+i \\ 2-i & 1 \end{bmatrix}$$

is a _____.

The entries on the main diagonal (top left to bottom right) of any _____ are necessarily real. A matrix that has only real entries is Hermitian if and only if it is a symmetric matrix, i.e., if it is symmetric with respect to the main diagonal.

- a. Permutation matrix
- b. Hermitian matrix
- c. Levinson recursion
- d. Symplectic matrix

34. In mathematics, an _____ is the finite or bounded case of a conic section, the geometric shape that results from cutting a circular conical or cylindrical surface with an oblique plane . It is also the locus of all points of the plane whose distances to two fixed points add to the same constant.

Ellipses also arise as images of a circle or a sphere under parallel projection, and some cases of perspective projection.

- a. ADE classification
- b. AKS primality test
- c. Ellipse
- d. Abelian P-root group

Chapter 5. EIGENVALUES AND EIGENVECTORS

35. In mathematics, particularly linear algebra and functional analysis, the _____ is any of a number of results about linear operators or about matrices. In broad terms the _____ provides conditions under which an operator or a matrix can be diagonalized (that is, represented as a diagonal matrix in some basis.) This concept of diagonalization is relatively straightforward for operators on finite-dimensional spaces, but requires some modification for operators on infinite-dimensional spaces.
    a. Spectral radius
    b. Spectral geometry
    c. Spectral asymmetry
    d. Spectral theorem

36. A complex square matrix A is a _____ if

    A*A=AA*

    where A* is the conjugate transpose of A. That is, a matrix is normal if it commutes with its conjugate transpose.

    If A is a real matrix, then A*=A^T; it is normal if A^{T}A = AA^T.

    Normality is a convenient test for diagonalizability: every _____ can be converted to a diagonal matrix by a unitary transform, and every matrix which can be made diagonal by a unitary transform is also normal, but finding the desired transform requires much more work than simply testing to see whether the matrix is normal.

    a. Main diagonal
    b. Duplication matrix
    c. Hamiltonian matrix
    d. Normal matrix

37. In mathematics, a _____ is an n by n complex matrix U satisfying the condition

$$U^*U = UU^* = I_n$$

where I_n is the identity matrix and U^* is the conjugate transpose (also called the Hermitian adjoint) of U. Note this condition says that a matrix U is unitary if and only if it has an inverse which is equal to its conjugate transpose U^*

$$U^{-1} = U^*$$

A _____ in which all entries are real is the same thing as an orthogonal matrix. Just as an orthogonal matrix G preserves the (real) inner product of two real vectors,

$$\langle Gx, Gy \rangle = \langle x, y \rangle$$

so also a _____ U satisfies

$$\langle Ux, Uy \rangle = \langle x, y \rangle$$

for all complex vectors x and y, where $\langle \cdot, \cdot \rangle$ stands now for the standard inner product on C^n. If U is an n by n matrix then the following are all equivalent conditions:

1. U is unitary
2. U^* is unitary
3. the columns of U form an orthonormal basis of C^n with respect to this inner product
4. the rows of U form an orthonormal basis of C^n with respect to this inner product
5. U is an isometry with respect to the norm from this inner product

It follows from the isometry property that all eigenvalues of a _____ are complex numbers of absolute value 1 (i.e., they lie on the unit circle centered at 0 in the complex plane.) The same is true for the determinant.

a. Integer matrix
b. Unimodular matrix
c. Unistochastic matrix
d. Unitary matrix

38. In mathematics, there are several meanings of _____ depending on the subject.

A _____, usually denoted by ° (the _____ symbol), is a measurement of plane angle, representing $\frac{1}{360}$ of a full rotation. When that angle is with respect to a reference meridian, it indicates a location along a great circle of a sphere, such as Earth , Mars, or the celestial sphere.

a. Degree
b. Relation algebra
c. Median algebra
d. Symmetric difference

Chapter 5. EIGENVALUES AND EIGENVECTORS

39. The _____ of an m-by-n matrix with real entries is the subspace of R^n generated by the row vectors of the matrix. Its dimension is equal to the rank of the matrix and is at most min(m,n.)

The column space of an m-by-n matrix with real entries is the subspace of R^m generated by the column vectors of the matrix.

   a. Differential graded algebra
   b. Row space
   c. Restriction of scalars
   d. Goodman-Nguyen-van Fraassen algebra

40. In linear algebra, a _____ is a special kind of Toeplitz matrix where each row vector is rotated one element to the right relative to the preceding row vector. In numerical analysis circulant matrices are important because they are diagonalized by a discrete Fourier transform, and hence linear equations that contain them may be quickly solved using a fast Fourier transform. They can be interpreted analytically as the integral kernel of a convolution operator on the cyclic group ☒ > In cryptography, a _____ is used in the MixColumns step of the Advanced Encryption Standard.
   a. Circulant matrix
   b. Minimum degree algorithm
   c. Pentadiagonal matrix
   d. Hilbert matrix

41. In mathematics and, in particular, functional analysis, _____ is a mathematical operation on two functions f and g, producing a third function that is typically viewed as a modified version of one of the original functions. _____ is similar to cross-correlation. It has applications that include statistics, computer vision, image and signal processing, electrical engineering, and differential equations.
   a. 2-bridge knot
   b. -module
   c. -equivalence
   d. Convolution

42. In mathematics, a _____ is a basic technique used to simplify problems in which the original variables are replaced with new ones; the new and old variables being related in some specified way. The intent is that the problem expressed in new variables may be simpler, or else equivalent to a better understood problem.

Chapter 5. EIGENVALUES AND EIGENVECTORS

A very simple example of a useful variable change can be seen in the problem of finding the roots of the eighth order polynomial:

$$x^8 + 3x^4 + 2 = 0$$

Eighth order polynomial equations are generally impossible to solve in terms of elementary functions.

a. Quadratic equation
b. FOIL rule
c. Difference of two squares
d. Change of variables

43. In linear algebra, two n-by-n matrices A and B are called _____ if

$$B = P^{-1}AP$$

for some invertible n-by-n matrix P. _____ matrices represent the same linear transformation under two different bases, with P being the change of basis matrix.

The matrix P is sometimes called a similarity transformation. In the context of matrix groups, similarity is sometimes referred to as conjugacy, with _____ matrices being conjugate.

a. Zero matrix
b. Skew-symmetric
c. Cartan matrix
d. Similar

44. If B(x, x) ≥ 0 for all x, B is said to be positive _____. Negative _____ bilinear forms are defined similarly.

As an example, let $V=R^2$, and consider the bilinear form

$B(x,y) = c_1 x_1 y_1 + c_2 x_2 y_2$

where $x = (x_1, x_2)$, $y = (y_1, y_2)$, and c_1 and c_2 are constants.

Chapter 5. EIGENVALUES AND EIGENVECTORS

a. 2-bridge knot
b. -module
c. -equivalence
d. Semidefinite

45. A _____ is a symbol that stands for a value that may vary; the term usually occurs in opposition to constant, which is a symbol for a non-varying value, i.e. completely fixed or fixed in the context of use. The concepts of constants and variables are fundamental to all modern mathematics, science, engineering, and computer programming.

Much of the basic theory for which we use variables today, such as school geometry and algebra, was developed thousands of years ago, but the use of symbolic formulae and variables is only several hundreds of years old.

a. -module
b. 2-bridge knot
c. -equivalence
d. Variable

46. In linear algebra, a basis for a vector space of dimension n is a sequence of n vectors $a_1, ..., a_n$ with the property that every vector in the space can be expressed uniquely as a linear combination of the basis vectors. Since it is often desirable to work with more than one basis for a vector space, it is of fundamental importance in linear algebra to be able to easily transform coordinate-wise representations of vectors and linear transformations taken with respect to one basis to their equivalent representations with respect to another basis. Such a transformation is called a _____.
a. Field of values
b. Generalized singular value decomposition
c. Split-complex number
d. Change of basis

47. In linear algebra, a _____ is a set of vectors that, in a linear combination, can represent every vector in a given vector space or free module, and such that no element of the set can be represented as a linear combination of the others. In other words, a _____ is a linearly independent spanning set.
a. Supergroup
b. Chirality
c. Minor
d. Basis

Chapter 5. EIGENVALUES AND EIGENVECTORS

48. In the mathematical discipline of linear algebra, a _____ is a special kind of square matrix where the entries either below or above the main diagonal are zero. Because matrix equations with triangular matrices are easier to solve they are very important in numerical analysis. The LU decomposition gives an algorithm to decompose any invertible matrix A into a normed lower triangle matrix L and an upper triangle matrix U.
   a. Triangular matrix
   b. Diagonally dominant
   c. Hilbert matrix
   d. Circulant matrix

49. In linear algebra, two vectors in an inner product space are _____ if they are orthogonal and both of unit length. A set of vectors form an _____ set if all vectors in the set are mutually orthogonal and all of unit length. An _____ set which forms a basis is called an _____ basis.
   a. Invertible matrix
   b. Orthonormal
   c. Elementary matrix
   d. Overdetermined

50. In mathematics, an element x of a ring R is called _____ if there exists some positive integer n such that $x^n = 0$.

The term was introduced by Benjamin Peirce in the context of elements of an algebra that vanish when raised to a power.

- This definition can be applied in particular to square matrices. The matrix

$$A = \begin{pmatrix} 0 & 1 & 0 \\ 0 & 0 & 1 \\ 0 & 0 & 0 \end{pmatrix}$$

is _____ because $A^3 = 0$. See _____ matrix for more.

   a. Nilpotent
   b. Ring of integers
   c. Product ring
   d. Hochschild homology

Chapter 6. POSITIVE DEFINITE MATRICES

1. In a totally ordered set all elements are mutually comparable, so such a set can have at most one minimal element and at most one maximal element. Then, due to mutual comparability, the minimal element will also be the least element and the maximal element will also be the greatest element. Thus in a totally ordered set we can simply use the terms _____ and maximum.

   a. 2-bridge knot
   b. -equivalence
   c. -module
   d. Minimum

2. _____ is definite, that is, has a real value with the same sign (positive or negative) for all non-zero x. According to that sign, B is called positive definite or _____. If Q takes both positive and negative values, the bilinear form B is called indefinite.

   a. -equivalence
   b. Negative definite
   c. -module
   d. 2-bridge knot

3. If $B(x, x) \geq 0$ for all x, B is said to be positive _____. Negative _____ bilinear forms are defined similarly.

   As an example, let $V=R^2$, and consider the bilinear form

   $$B(x,y) = c_1 x_1 y_1 + c_2 x_2 y_2$$

   where $x = (x_1, x_2)$, $y = (y_1, y_2)$, and c_1 and c_2 are constants.

   a. 2-bridge knot
   b. -module
   c. -equivalence
   d. Semidefinite

4. _____ is a concept that permeates much of inferential statistics and descriptive statistics. More properly, it is 'the sum of the squared deviations'. Mathematically, it is an unscaled, or unadjusted measure of dispersion (also called variability.)

   a. -module
   b. -equivalence
   c. 2-bridge knot
   d. Sum of squares

Chapter 6. POSITIVE DEFINITE MATRICES

5. In mathematics, a _____ is a point in the domain of a function of two variables which is a stationary point but not a local extremum. At such a point, in general, the surface resembles a saddle that curves up in one direction, and curves down in a different direction (like a mountain pass.) In terms of contour lines, a _____ can be recognized, in general, by a contour that appears to intersect itself.
   a. Gauss map
   b. Ridge
   c. Weingarten equations
   d. Saddle point

6. In mathematics, a _____ is a matrix formed by selecting certain rows and columns from a bigger matrix. That is, as an array, it is cut down to those entries constrained by row and column.

For example

$$\mathbf{A} = \begin{bmatrix} a_{11} & a_{12} & a_{13} & a_{14} \\ a_{21} & a_{22} & a_{23} & a_{24} \\ a_{31} & a_{32} & a_{33} & a_{34} \end{bmatrix}.$$

Then

$$\mathbf{A}[1,2;1,3,4] = \begin{bmatrix} a_{11} & a_{13} & a_{14} \\ a_{21} & a_{23} & a_{24} \end{bmatrix}$$

is a _____ of A formed by rows 1,2 and columns 1,3,4.

   a. Lie product formula
   b. Smith normal form
   c. Quasideterminant
   d. Submatrix

7. For each eigenvector of a linear transformation, there is a corresponding scalar value called an _____ for that vector, which determines the amount the eigenvector is scaled under the linear transformation. For example, an _____ of +2 means that the eigenvector is doubled in length and points in the same direction. An _____ of +1 means that the eigenvector is unchanged, while an _____ of −1 means that the eigenvector is reversed in sense.
   a. Eigenvalue
   b. AKS primality test
   c. Abelian P-root group
   d. ADE classification

Chapter 6. POSITIVE DEFINITE MATRICES

8. An _____ is a type of quadric surface that is a higher dimensional analogue of an ellipse. The equation of a standard axis-aligned _____ body in an xyz-Cartesian coordinate system is

$$\frac{x^2}{a^2} + \frac{y^2}{b^2} + \frac{z^2}{c^2} = 1$$

where a and b are the equatorial radii (along the x and y axes) and c is the polar radius (along the z-axis), all of which are fixed positive real numbers determining the shape of the _____.

More generally, a not-necessarily-axis-aligned _____ is defined by the equation

$$\mathbf{x}^T A \mathbf{x} = 1$$

where A is a symmetric positive definite matrix and x is a vector.

   a. AKS primality test
   b. Ellipsoid
   c. ADE classification
   d. Abelian P-root group

9. In mathematics, a _____ of a number x is a number r such that $r^2 = x$, or, in other words, a number r whose square (the result of multiplying the number by itself) is x.

Every non-negative real number x has a unique non-negative _____, called the principal _____, which is denoted with a radical symbol as $\sqrt{x}$, or, using exponent notation, as $x^{1/2}$. For example, the principal _____ of 9 is 3, denoted $\sqrt{9} = 3$, because $3^2 = 3 \times 3 = 9$.

   a. -equivalence
   b. 2-bridge knot
   c. -module
   d. Square root

10. In mathematics, a _____ of a number x is any number which, when repeatedly multiplied by itself, eventually yields x:

$$r \times r \times \cdots \times r = x.$$

Chapter 6. POSITIVE DEFINITE MATRICES

In terms of exponentiation, r is a _____ of x if

$$r^n = x$$

for some positive integer n. For example, 2 is a _____ of 16 since $2^4 = 2 \times 2 \times 2 \times 2 = 16$.

The number n is called the degree of the _____.

a. Rationalisation
b. Root
c. Difference of two squares
d. Cubic function

11. In mathematics, the Cauchy-_____ the Cauchy inequality is a useful inequality encountered in many different settings, such as linear algebra applied to vectors, in analysis applied to infinite series and integration of products, and in probability theory, applied to variances and covariances. The general formulation of the Heisenberg uncertainty principle is derived using the Cauchy-_____ in the Hilbert space of pure quantum states.

The inequality for sums was published by , while the corresponding inequality for integrals was first stated by and rediscovered by

a. -module
b. 2-bridge knot
c. -equivalence
d. Schwarz inequality

12. In mathematics, an _____ is a statement about the relative size or order of two objects, or about whether they are the same or not

- The notation a < b means that a is less than b.
- The notation a > b means that a is greater than b.
- The notation a ≠ b means that a is not equal to b, but does not say that one is bigger than the other or even that they can be compared in size.

In all these cases, a is not equal to b, hence, '_____'.

Chapter 6. POSITIVE DEFINITE MATRICES

These relations are known as strict _____

- The notation a ≤ b means that a is less than or equal to b (or, equivalently, not greater than b);
- The notation a ≥ b means that a is greater than or equal to b (or, equivalently, not smaller than b);

An additional use of the notation is to show that one quantity is much greater than another, normally by several orders of magnitude.

- The notation a ≪ b means that a is much less than b.
- The notation a ≫ b means that a is much greater than b.

If the sense of the _____ is the same for all values of the variables for which its members are defined, then the _____ is called an 'absolute' or 'unconditional' _____. If the sense of an _____ holds only for certain values of the variables involved, but is reversed or destroyed for other values of the variables, it is called a conditional _____.

One can apply the same algebraic operations to inequalities as one would apply for solving equalities. For example, to find x for the _____ 10x > 20 one would divide 20 by 10 to obtain x > 2.

  a. ADE classification
  b. Inequality
  c. AKS primality test
  d. Abelian P-root group

13. In mathematics, a _____ is a basic technique used to simplify problems in which the original variables are replaced with new ones; the new and old variables being related in some specified way. The intent is that the problem expressed in new variables may be simpler, or else equivalent to a better understood problem.

A very simple example of a useful variable change can be seen in the problem of finding the roots of the eighth order polynomial:

$$x^8 + 3x^4 + 2 = 0$$

Eighth order polynomial equations are generally impossible to solve in terms of elementary functions.

  a. FOIL rule
  b. Difference of two squares
  c. Quadratic equation
  d. Change of variables

Chapter 6. POSITIVE DEFINITE MATRICES

14. In topology, two continuous functions from one topological space to another are called homotopic if one can be 'continuously deformed' into the other, such a deformation being called a _____ between the two functions. An outstanding use of _____ is the definition of _____ groups and cohomotopy groups, important invariants in algebraic topology.

In practice, there are technical difficulties in using homotopies with certain pathological spaces.

   a. Freudenthal suspension theorem
   b. Simple-homotopy equivalence
   c. Homotopy
   d. J-homomorphism

15. A _____ is a symbol that stands for a value that may vary; the term usually occurs in opposition to constant, which is a symbol for a non-varying value, i.e. completely fixed or fixed in the context of use. The concepts of constants and variables are fundamental to all modern mathematics, science, engineering, and computer programming.

Much of the basic theory for which we use variables today, such as school geometry and algebra, was developed thousands of years ago, but the use of symbolic formulae and variables is only several hundreds of years old.

   a. 2-bridge knot
   b. -module
   c. -equivalence
   d. Variable

16. In numerical linear algebra, the _____ is an eigenvalue algorithm; that is, a procedure to calculate the eigenvalues and eigenvectors of a matrix. The QR transformation was developed in 1961 by John G.F. Francis (England) and by Vera N. Kublanovskaya (USSR), working independently. The basic idea is to perform a QR decomposition, writing the matrix as a product of an orthogonal matrix and an upper triangular matrix, multiply the factors in the other order, and iterate.
   a. -module
   b. 2-bridge knot
   c. QR algorithm
   d. -equivalence

17. In mathematics, a _____ is a rectangular array of numbers. This way, matrices can record data that depend on multiple parameters. In particular they are used to keep track of the coefficients of multiple linear equations. Matrices are closely connected to linear transformations, which are higher-dimensional analogs of linear functions, i.e., functions of the form f(x) = c Â· x, where c is a constant. This map corresponds to a _____ with one row and column, with entry c. In addition to a number of elementary, entrywise operations such as _____ addition a key notion is _____ multiplication, which displays a number of features not encountered in numbers; for example, products of matrices depend on the order of the factors, unlike products of real numbers, say, where c Â· d = d Â· c for any two numbers c and d.

a. Heap
b. Matrix
c. Commutativity
d. Polynomial expression

18. In algebraic topology, a simplicial k-_____ is a formal linear combination of k-simplices.

Integration is defined on chains by taking the linear combination of integrals over the simplices in the _____ with coefficients typically integers. The set of all k-chains forms a group and the sequence of these groups is called a _____ complex.

a. Chain
b. Combinatorial topology
c. Bockstein homomorphism
d. Tesseract

19. In mathematics, for a given complex Hermitian matrix A and nonzero vector x, the _____ R(A,x) is defined as:

$$\frac{x^* A x}{x^* x}.$$

For real matrices and vectors, the condition of being Hermitian reduces to that of being symmetric, and the conjugate transpose x* to the usual transpose x'. Note that R(A,cx) = R(A,x) for any real scalar c. Recall that a Hermitian (or real symmetric) matrix has real eigenvalues.

a. Rayleigh quotient
b. Vectorization
c. Projection-valued measure
d. Reality structure

20. The method of _____ is used to approximately solve overdetermined systems, i.e. systems of equations in which there are more equations than unknowns. _____ is often applied in statistical contexts, particularly regression analysis.

_____ can be interpreted as a method of fitting data.

a. -equivalence
b. Least squares
c. 2-bridge knot
d. -module

21. The _____ is a numerical technique for finding approximate solutions of partial differential equations (PDE) as well as of integral equations. The solution approach is based either on eliminating the differential equation completely (steady state problems), or rendering the PDE into an approximating system of ordinary differential equations, which are then numerically integrated using standard techniques such as Euler's method, Runge-Kutta, etc.

In solving partial differential equations, the primary challenge is to create an equation that approximates the equation to be studied, but is numerically stable, meaning that errors in the input data and intermediate calculations do not accumulate and cause the resulting output to be meaningless.

a. -equivalence
b. 2-bridge knot
c. -module
d. Finite element method

Chapter 7. COMPUTATIONS WITH MATRICES

1. In numerical analysis, the _____ associated with a problem is a measure of that problem's amenability to digital computation, that is, how numerically well-conditioned the problem is. A problem with a low _____ is said to be well-conditioned, while a problem with a high _____ is said to be ill-conditioned.

   For example, the _____ associated with the linear equation Ax = b gives a bound on how inaccurate the solution x will be after approximate solution.

   a. Bernstein polynomial
   b. -module
   c. -equivalence
   d. Condition number

2. In linear algebra, functional analysis and related areas of mathematics, a _____ is a function that assigns a strictly positive length or size to all vectors in a vector space, other than the zero vector. A seminorm (or pseudonorm), on the other hand, is allowed to assign zero length to some non-zero vectors.

   A simple example is the 2-dimensional Euclidean space R^2 equipped with the Euclidean _____.

   a. Quasinorm
   b. -equivalence
   c. -module
   d. Norm

3. In mathematics, a _____ is a rectangular array of numbers. This way, matrices can record data that depend on multiple parameters. In particular they are used to keep track of the coefficients of multiple linear equations. Matrices are closely connected to linear transformations, which are higher-dimensional analogs of linear functions, i.e., functions of the form f(x) = c Â· x, where c is a constant. This map corresponds to a _____ with one row and column, with entry c. In addition to a number of elementary, entrywise operations such as _____ addition a key notion is _____ multiplication, which displays a number of features not encountered in numbers; for example, products of matrices depend on the order of the factors, unlike products of real numbers, say, where c Â· d = d Â· c for any two numbers c and d.
   a. Heap
   b. Commutativity
   c. Polynomial expression
   d. Matrix

4. In mathematics, in particular functional analysis, the _____, or s-numbers of a compact operator T acting on a Hilbert space are defined as the eigenvalues of the operator $\sqrt{T^*T}$ (where T^* denotes the adjoint of T and the square root is taken in the operator sense.) The _____ are nonnegative real numbers, usually listed in decreasing order $s_1(T)$, $s_2(T)$, ...

a. -module
b. 2-bridge knot
c. Singular values
d. -equivalence

5. A _____ is one of the basic shapes of geometry: a polygon with three corners or vertices and three sides or edges which are line segments. A _____ with vertices A, B, and C is denoted ABC.

In Euclidean geometry any three non-collinear points determine a unique _____ and a unique plane (i.e. a two-dimensional Euclidean space.)

a. -equivalence
b. -module
c. 2-bridge knot
d. Triangle

6. In mathematics, the _____ states that for any triangle, the length of a given side must be less than the sum of the other two sides but greater than the difference between the two sides.

In Euclidean geometry and some other geometries this is a theorem. In the Euclidean case, in both the less than or equal to and greater than or equal to statements, equality occurs only if the triangle has a 180° angle and two 0° angles, as shown in the bottom example in the image to the right.

a. -module
b. 2-bridge knot
c. -equivalence
d. Triangle inequality

7. In mathematics, an _____ is a statement about the relative size or order of two objects, or about whether they are the same or not

- The notation a < b means that a is less than b.
- The notation a > b means that a is greater than b.
- The notation a ≠ b means that a is not equal to b, but does not say that one is bigger than the other or even that they can be compared in size.

In all these cases, a is not equal to b, hence, '_____'.

Chapter 7. COMPUTATIONS WITH MATRICES

These relations are known as strict _____

- The notation a ≤ b means that a is less than or equal to b (or, equivalently, not greater than b);
- The notation a ≥ b means that a is greater than or equal to b (or, equivalently, not smaller than b);

An additional use of the notation is to show that one quantity is much greater than another, normally by several orders of magnitude.

- The notation a ≪ b means that a is much less than b.
- The notation a ≫ b means that a is much greater than b.

If the sense of the _____ is the same for all values of the variables for which its members are defined, then the _____ is called an 'absolute' or 'unconditional' _____. If the sense of an _____ holds only for certain values of the variables involved, but is reversed or destroyed for other values of the variables, it is called a conditional _____.

One can apply the same algebraic operations to inequalities as one would apply for solving equalities. For example, to find x for the _____ 10x > 20 one would divide 20 by 10 to obtain x > 2.

a. Abelian P-root group
b. AKS primality test
c. ADE classification
d. Inequality

8. For each eigenvector of a linear transformation, there is a corresponding scalar value called an _____ for that vector, which determines the amount the eigenvector is scaled under the linear transformation. For example, an _____ of +2 means that the eigenvector is doubled in length and points in the same direction. An _____ of +1 means that the eigenvector is unchanged, while an _____ of −1 means that the eigenvector is reversed in sense.

a. AKS primality test
b. ADE classification
c. Abelian P-root group
d. Eigenvalue

9. In mathematics, the _____ is an eigenvalue algorithm: given a matrix A, the algorithm will produce a number λ (the eigenvalue) and a nonzero vector v (the eigenvector), such that Av = λv.

The _____ is a very simple algorithm. It does not compute a matrix decomposition, and hence it can be used when A is a very large sparse matrix.

Chapter 7. COMPUTATIONS WITH MATRICES

a. 2-bridge knot
b. -module
c. -equivalence
d. Power iteration

10. In mathematics and group theory, a _____ system for the action of a group G on a set X is a partition of X that is G-invariant. In terms of the associated equivalence relation on X, G-invariance means that

   $x \equiv y$ implies $gx \equiv gy$

for all g in G and all x, y in X. The action of G on X determines a natural action of G on any _____ system for X.

Each element of the _____ system is called a _____.

a. Symmetric group
b. Parker vector
c. Frobenius group
d. Block

11. In mathematics, for a given complex Hermitian matrix A and nonzero vector x, the _____ R(A,x) is defined as:

$$\frac{x^* A x}{x^* x}.$$

For real matrices and vectors, the condition of being Hermitian reduces to that of being symmetric, and the conjugate transpose x^* to the usual transpose x'. Note that R(A,cx) = R(A,x) for any real scalar c. Recall that a Hermitian (or real symmetric) matrix has real eigenvalues.

a. Reality structure
b. Projection-valued measure
c. Rayleigh quotient
d. Vectorization

12. In linear algebra, a _____ is a linear transformation that squares to the identity ($R^2 = I$, where R is in K dimensional space), also known as an involution in the general linear group. In addition to reflections across hyperplanes, the class of general reflections includes point reflections, reflections across subspaces of intermediate dimension, and non-orthogonal reflections.

A _____ over a hyperplane in an inner product space is necessarily symmetric, but a general _____ need not be as the example $\begin{bmatrix} 1 & 0 \\ 1 & -1 \end{bmatrix}$ shows.

a. Homomorphic secret sharing
b. Reflection
c. Morphism
d. Shear mappings

13. In linear algebra, the _____ is an important factorization of a rectangular real or complex matrix, with several applications in signal processing and statistics. Applications which employ the _____ include computing the pseudoinverse, least squares fitting of data, matrix approximation, and determining the rank, range and null space of a matrix.

Suppose M is an m-by-n matrix whose entries come from the field K, which is either the field of real numbers or the field of complex numbers.

a. 2-bridge knot
b. -module
c. -equivalence
d. Singular value decomposition

14. In numerical linear algebra, the _____ is an eigenvalue algorithm; that is, a procedure to calculate the eigenvalues and eigenvectors of a matrix. The QR transformation was developed in 1961 by John G.F. Francis (England) and by Vera N. Kublanovskaya (USSR), working independently. The basic idea is to perform a QR decomposition, writing the matrix as a product of an orthogonal matrix and an upper triangular matrix, multiply the factors in the other order, and iterate.

a. 2-bridge knot
b. -module
c. QR algorithm
d. -equivalence

15. In mathematics, _____ or factoring is the decomposition of an object ' href='/wiki/Matrix_(mathematics)'>matrix) into a product of other objects, or factors, which when multiplied together give the original. For example, the number 15 factors into primes as 3 × 5, and the polynomial $x^2 - 4$ factors as $(x - 2)(x + 2)$. In all cases, a product of simpler objects is obtained.

Chapter 7. COMPUTATIONS WITH MATRICES

a. Factorization
b. -equivalence
c. 2-bridge knot
d. -module

16. In mathematics, a _____ is a flat surface. Planes can arise as subspaces of some higher dimensional space, as with the walls of a room, or they may enjoy an independent existence in their own right, as in the setting of Euclidean geometry
    a. Similarity
    b. Plane
    c. -equivalence
    d. -module

17. In geometry and linear algebra, a _____ is a transformation in a plane or in space that describes the motion of a rigid body around a fixed point. A _____ is different from a translation, which has no fixed points, and from a reflection, which 'flips' the bodies it is transforming. A _____ and the above-mentioned transformations are isometries; they leave the distance between any two points unchanged after the transformation.
    a. Shear mappings
    b. Real matrices
    c. Rotation
    d. Reflection

18. In linear algebra and numerical analysis, a _____ P of a matrix A is a matrix such that $P^{-1}A$ has a smaller condition number than A. Preconditioners are useful when using an iterative method to solve a large, sparse linear system

$$Ax = b$$

for x since the rate of convergence for most iterative linear solvers degrades as the condition number of a matrix increases. Instead of solving the original linear system above, one may solve either the left preconditioned system

$$P^{-1}Ax = P^{-1}b,$$

via the two solves

$$c = P^{-1}b, \qquad (P^{-1}A)x = c,$$

or the right preconditioned system

$$AP^{-1}Px = b,$$

via the two solves

$$(AP^{-1})y = b, \qquad x = P^{-1}y,$$

which are both equivalent to solving the original system so long as the _____ matrix P is nonsingular.

The goal of this preconditioned system is to reduce the condition number of the left or right preconditioned system matrix

$$P^{-1}A,$$

or

$$AP^{-1},$$

respectively.

a. Preconditioner
b. -module
c. 2-bridge knot
d. -equivalence

19. In mathematics, the _____ of a matrix or a bounded linear operator is the supremum among the absolute values of the elements in its spectrum, which is sometimes denoted by ρ(Â·.)

Let $\lambda_1, ..., \lambda_s$ be the (real or complex) eigenvalues of a matrix $A \in C^{n \times n}$. Then its _____ ρ(A) is defined as:

ρ(A): = max$_i$(| λ_i |)

The following lemma shows a simple yet useful upper bound for the _____ of a matrix:

Chapter 7. COMPUTATIONS WITH MATRICES

Lemma: Let $A \in C^{n \times n}$ be a complex-valued matrix, $\rho(A)$ its _____ and $||\hat{A}\cdot||$ a consistent matrix norm; then, for each $k \in \mathbb{N}$:

$$\rho(A) \leq \|A^k\|^{1/k}, \forall k \in \mathbb{N}.$$

Proof: Let (v, λ) be an eigenvector-eigenvalue pair for a matrix A. By the sub-multiplicative property of the matrix norm, we get:

$$|\lambda|^k \|\mathbf{v}\| = \|\lambda^k \mathbf{v}\| = \|A^k \mathbf{v}\| \leq \|A^k\| \cdot \|\mathbf{v}\|$$

and since $v \neq 0$ for each λ we have

$$|\lambda|^k \leq \|A^k\|$$

and therefore

$$\rho(A) \leq \|A^k\|^{1/k} \quad \square$$

The _____ is closely related to the behaviour of the convergence of the power sequence of a matrix; namely, the following theorem holds:

Theorem: Let $A \in C^{n \times n}$ be a complex-valued matrix and $\rho(A)$ its _____; then

$$\lim_{k \to \infty} A^k = 0$$

if and only if $\rho(A) < 1$.

Moreover, if $\rho(A) > 1$, $\|A^k\|$ is not bounded for increasing k values.

a. Spectral geometry
b. Spectral asymmetry
c. Spectral theorem
d. Spectral radius

20. In algebra, a _____ of an element in a quadratic extension field of a field K is its image under the unique non-identity automorphism of the extended field that fixes K. If the extension is generated by a square root of an element r of K, then the _____ of $a + b\sqrt{r}$ is $a - b\sqrt{r}$ for $a, b \in K$, and in particular in the case of the field C of complex numbers as an extension of the field R of real numbers (where r = − 1), the complex _____ of a + bi is a − bi.

Forming the sum or product of any element of the extension field with its _____ always gives an element of K. This can be used to rewrite a quotient of numbers in the extended field so that the denominator lies in K, by multiplying numerator and denominator by the _____ of the denominator. This process is called rationalization of the denominator, in particular if K is the field Q of rational numbers.

a. K-theory
b. Field arithmetic
c. Digital root
d. Conjugate

21. In mathematics, the _____ may be used to bound the spectrum of a square matrix. It was first published by the Belarusian mathematician Semyon Aranovich Gershgorin in 1931. The spelling of S. A. Gershgorin's name has been transliterated in several different ways, including GerÅÂ¡gorin, Gerschgorin, Gershgorin and Hershhorn/Hirschhorn, the latter corresponding to the transliteration of the Yiddish spelling of his name, which is >×â€ ×â„¢×Â¨×Â©×â€ ×Â ÖÂ¸×Â¨×Å¸.

a. Malgrange preparation theorem
b. Structure theorem for finitely generated modules over a principal ideal domain
c. Lattice theorem
d. Gershgorin circle theorem

22. In mathematics, a matrix is said to be _____ if in every row of the matrix, the magnitude of the diagonal entry in that row is larger than or equal to the sum of the magnitudes of all the other (non-diagonal) entries in that row, and if in at least one row of the matrix, the magnitude of the diagonal entry in that row is strictly larger than the sum of the magnitudes of all the other (non-diagonal) entries in that row. More precisely, the matrix A is _____ if

$$|a_{ii}| \geq \sum_{j \neq i} |a_{ij}| \quad \text{for all } i, \quad |a_{ii}| > \sum_{j \neq i} |a_{ij}| \quad \text{for at least one } i,$$

<_____>

where a_{ij} denotes the entry in the ith row and jth column. If the strictly greater than equality is true for all rows (all values of i), then the matrix is called strictly _____.

a. Triangular matrix
b. Minimum degree algorithm
c. Diagonally dominant
d. Circulant matrix

Chapter 8. LINEAR PROGRAMMING AND GAME THEORY

1. In mathematics, _____ is a technique for optimization of a linear objective function, subject to linear equality and linear inequality constraints. Informally, _____ determines the way to achieve the best outcome (such as maximum profit or lowest cost) in a given mathematical model and given some list of requirements represented as linear equations.

More formally, given a polytope (for example, a polygon or a polyhedron), and a real-valued affine function

$$f(x_1, x_2, \ldots, x_n) = c_1 x_1 + c_2 x_2 + \cdots + c_n x_n + d$$

defined on this polytope, a _____ method will find a point in the polytope where this function has the smallest (or largest) value.

  a. -module
  b. 2-bridge knot
  c. -equivalence
  d. Linear programming

2. In mathematics, an _____ is a statement about the relative size or order of two objects, or about whether they are the same or not

  - The notation a < b means that a is less than b.
  - The notation a > b means that a is greater than b.
  - The notation a ≠ b means that a is not equal to b, but does not say that one is bigger than the other or even that they can be compared in size.

In all these cases, a is not equal to b, hence, '_____'.

These relations are known as strict _____

  - The notation a ≤ b means that a is less than or equal to b (or, equivalently, not greater than b);
  - The notation a ≥ b means that a is greater than or equal to b (or, equivalently, not smaller than b);

An additional use of the notation is to show that one quantity is much greater than another, normally by several orders of magnitude.

  - The notation a ≪ b means that a is much less than b.
  - The notation a ≫ b means that a is much greater than b.

If the sense of the _____ is the same for all values of the variables for which its members are defined, then the _____ is called an 'absolute' or 'unconditional' _____. If the sense of an _____ holds only for certain values of the variables involved, but is reversed or destroyed for other values of the variables, it is called a conditional _____.

One can apply the same algebraic operations to inequalities as one would apply for solving equalities. For example, to find x for the _____ 10x > 20 one would divide 20 by 10 to obtain x > 2.

Chapter 8. LINEAR PROGRAMMING AND GAME THEORY

   a. Inequality
   b. ADE classification
   c. Abelian P-root group
   d. AKS primality test

3. An unrelated, but similarly named method is the Nelder-Mead method or downhill _____ due to Nelder ' Mead (1965) and is a numerical method for optimizing many-dimensional unconstrained problems, belonging to the more general class of search algorithms.

In both cases, the method uses the concept of a simplex, which is a polytope of N + 1 vertices in N dimensions: a line segment in one dimension, a triangle in two dimensions, a tetrahedron in three-dimensional space and so forth.

A system of linear inequalities defines a polytope as a feasible region.
   a. -module
   b. -equivalence
   c. Simplex method
   d. 2-bridge knot

4. A _____ is a symbol that stands for a value that may vary; the term usually occurs in opposition to constant, which is a symbol for a non-varying value, i.e. completely fixed or fixed in the context of use. The concepts of constants and variables are fundamental to all modern mathematics, science, engineering, and computer programming.

Much of the basic theory for which we use variables today, such as school geometry and algebra, was developed thousands of years ago, but the use of symbolic formulae and variables is only several hundreds of years old.

   a. -module
   b. Variable
   c. -equivalence
   d. 2-bridge knot

5. In mathematics, _____(F_n) is the outer automorphism group of a free group on n generators. These groups play an important role in geometric group theory.

_____(F_n) acts geometrically on a cell complex known as outer space, which can be thought of as the Teichmüller space for a bouquet of circles.

Chapter 8. LINEAR PROGRAMMING AND GAME THEORY

   a. ADE classification
   b. AKS primality test
   c. Abelian P-root group
   d. Out

6. In linear algebra and functional analysis, a _____ is a linear transformation P from a vector space to itself such that $P^2 = P$. It leaves its image unchanged. Though abstract, this definition of '_____' formalizes and generalizes the idea of graphical _____.
   a. C_0-semigroup
   b. Projection
   c. Convolution power
   d. Lumer-Phillips theorem

7. In algebra, a _____ of an element in a quadratic extension field of a field K is its image under the unique non-identity automorphism of the extended field that fixes K. If the extension is generated by a square root of an element r of K, then the _____ of $a + b\sqrt{r}$ is $a - b\sqrt{r}$ for $a, b \in K$, and in particular in the case of the field C of complex numbers as an extension of the field R of real numbers (where r = − 1), the complex _____ of a + bi is a − bi.

Forming the sum or product of any element of the extension field with its _____ always gives an element of K. This can be used to rewrite a quotient of numbers in the extended field so that the denominator lies in K, by multiplying numerator and denominator by the _____ of the denominator. This process is called rationalization of the denominator, in particular if K is the field Q of rational numbers.

   a. Conjugate
   b. Field arithmetic
   c. Digital root
   d. K-theory

8. In topology, especially algebraic topology, the _____ CX of a topological space X is the quotient space:

$$CX = (X \times I)/(X \times \{0\})$$

of the product of X with the unit interval I = [0, 1]. Intuitively we make X into a cylinder and collapse one end of the cylinder to a point.

If X sits inside Euclidean space, the _____ on X is homeomorphic to the union of lines from X to another point.

Chapter 8. LINEAR PROGRAMMING AND GAME THEORY

   a. Smash product
   b. Genus
   c. Cone
   d. Descent

9. A _____ is a concept in geometry. It is a higher-dimensional generalization of the concepts of a line in the plane and a plane in 3-dimensional space. The most familiar kinds of _____ are affine and linear hyperplanes; less familiar is the projective _____.
   a. Hyperplane
   b. Kodaira embedding theorem
   c. Cusp
   d. Polar homology

10. In mathematics, an _____ is a matrix that shows the relationship between two classes of objects. If the first class is X and the second is Y, the matrix has one row for each element of X and one column for each element of Y. The entry in row x and column y is 1 if x and y are related (called incident in this context) and 0 if they are not.
   a. ADE classification
   b. Abelian P-root group
   c. Incidence matrix
   d. AKS primality test

11. In mathematics, a _____ is a rectangular array of numbers. This way, matrices can record data that depend on multiple parameters. In particular they are used to keep track of the coefficients of multiple linear equations. Matrices are closely connected to linear transformations, which are higher-dimensional analogs of linear functions, i.e., functions of the form f(x) = c Â· x, where c is a constant. This map corresponds to a _____ with one row and column, with entry c. In addition to a number of elementary, entrywise operations such as _____ addition a key notion is _____ multiplication, which displays a number of features not encountered in numbers; for example, products of matrices depend on the order of the factors, unlike products of real numbers, say, where c Â· d = d Â· c for any two numbers c and d.
   a. Polynomial expression
   b. Heap
   c. Matrix
   d. Commutativity

12. In mathematics and group theory, a _____ system for the action of a group G on a set X is a partition of X that is G-invariant. In terms of the associated equivalence relation on X, G-invariance means that

   $x \equiv y$ implies $gx \equiv gy$

for all g in G and all x, y in X. The action of G on X determines a natural action of G on any _____ system for X.

Each element of the _____ system is called a _____.

a. Parker vector
b. Symmetric group
c. Frobenius group
d. Block

13. In mathematics, a _____ is a point in the domain of a function of two variables which is a stationary point but not a local extremum. At such a point, in general, the surface resembles a saddle that curves up in one direction, and curves down in a different direction (like a mountain pass.) In terms of contour lines, a _____ can be recognized, in general, by a contour that appears to intersect itself.
a. Weingarten equations
b. Ridge
c. Gauss map
d. Saddle point

14. In linear algebra, a _____ matrix is a square matrix A whose transpose is also its negative; that is, it satisfies the equation:

$$A^T = -A$$

or in component form, if $A = (a_{ij})$:

$$a_{ij} = -a_{ji} \text{ for all i and j.}$$

For example, the following matrix is _____:

$$\begin{bmatrix} 0 & 2 & -1 \\ -2 & 0 & -4 \\ 1 & 4 & 0 \end{bmatrix}.$$

Compare this with a symmetric matrix whose transpose is the same as the matrix

$$A^T = A,$$

or to an orthogonal matrix, the transpose of which is equal to its inverse:

$$A^T = A^{-1}.$$

Sums and scalar products of _____ matrices are again _____. Hence, the _____ matrices form a vector space. Its dimension is $\frac{n(n-1)}{2}$.

a. Duplication matrix
b. Complex Hadamard matrix
c. Bisymmetric matrix
d. Skew-symmetric

15. For each _____ of a linear transformation, there is a corresponding scalar value called an eigenvalue for that vector, which determines the amount the _____ is scaled under the linear transformation. For example, an eigenvalue of +2 means that the _____ is doubled in length and points in the same direction. An eigenvalue of +1 means that the _____ is unchanged, while an eigenvalue of −1 means that the _____ is reversed in sense.
a. AKS primality test
b. Abelian P-root group
c. ADE classification
d. Eigenvector

16. In mathematics, two vectors are _____ if they are perpendicular, i.e., they form a right angle. The word comes from the Greek ά½€ρθϊŒς , meaning 'straight', and γωνῖα (gonia), meaning 'angle'. For example, a subway and the street above, although they do not physically intersect, are _____ if they cross at a right angle.
a. Embedding
b. Orthogonal
c. Expression
d. Unital

17. In linear algebra, an _____ is a square matrix with real entries whose columns (or rows) are orthogonal unit vectors (i.e., orthonormal.) Equivalently, a matrix Q is orthogonal if its transpose is equal to its inverse:

$$Q^T Q = Q Q^T = I.$$

As a linear transformation, an _____ preserves the dot product of vectors, and therefore acts as an isometry of Euclidean space, such as a rotation or reflection.

The set of n × n orthogonal matrices forms a group O(n), known as the orthogonal group.

a. Unistochastic matrix
b. Alternating sign matrix
c. Unimodular matrix
d. Orthogonal matrix

18. In mathematics, in particular functional analysis, the _____, or s-numbers of a compact operator T acting on a Hilbert space are defined as the eigenvalues of the operator $\sqrt{T^*T}$ (where T* denotes the adjoint of T and the square root is taken in the operator sense.) The _____ are nonnegative real numbers, usually listed in decreasing order $s_1(T)$, $s_2(T)$, ...

a. -module
b. Singular values
c. -equivalence
d. 2-bridge knot

19. In linear algebra, the _____ is an important factorization of a rectangular real or complex matrix, with several applications in signal processing and statistics. Applications which employ the _____ include computing the pseudoinverse, least squares fitting of data, matrix approximation, and determining the rank, range and null space of a matrix.

Suppose M is an m-by-n matrix whose entries come from the field K, which is either the field of real numbers or the field of complex numbers.

a. -module
b. 2-bridge knot
c. -equivalence
d. Singular value decomposition

20. In mathematics, particularly in linear algebra and functional analysis, the _____ of a matrix or linear operator is a factorization analogous to the polar form of a nonzero complex number z

$$z = re^{i\theta}$$

where r is the absolute value of z (a positive real number), and $e^{i\theta}$ is called the complex sign of z.

The _____ of a complex matrix A is a matrix decomposition of the form

$$A = UP$$

where U is a unitary matrix and P is a positive-semidefinite Hermitian matrix. This decomposition always exists; and so long as A is invertible, it is unique, with P positive-definite.

   a. Positive definite function on a group
   b. Riesz-Thorin theorem
   c. Cholesky decomposition
   d. Polar decomposition

21. The column _____ of a matrix A is the maximal number of linearly independent columns of A. Likewise, the row _____ is the maximal number of linearly independent rows of A.

Since the column _____ and the row _____ are always equal, they are simply called the _____ of A. More abstractly, it is the dimension of the image of A. For the proofs, see, e.g., Murase (1960), Andrea ' Wong (1960), Williams ' Cater (1968), Mackiw (1995.) It is commonly denoted by either rk(A) or _____ A

   a. Generalized Pauli matrices
   b. Rank
   c. Split-complex number
   d. Schur complement

22. If $B(x, x) \geq 0$ for all x, B is said to be positive _____. Negative _____ bilinear forms are defined similarly.

As an example, let $V=R^2$, and consider the bilinear form

   $B(x,y) = c_1 x_1 y_1 + c_2 x_2 y_2$

where $x = (x_1, x_2)$, $y = (y_1, y_2)$, and c_1 and c_2 are constants.

   a. -equivalence
   b. 2-bridge knot
   c. Semidefinite
   d. -module

Chapter 8. LINEAR PROGRAMMING AND GAME THEORY

23. The method of _____ is used to approximately solve overdetermined systems, i.e. systems of equations in which there are more equations than unknowns. _____ is often applied in statistical contexts, particularly regression analysis.

_____ can be interpreted as a method of fitting data.

a. -equivalence
b. Least squares
c. -module
d. 2-bridge knot

24. In geometry and linear algebra, a _____ is a transformation in a plane or in space that describes the motion of a rigid body around a fixed point. A _____ is different from a translation, which has no fixed points, and from a reflection, which 'flips' the bodies it is transforming. A _____ and the above-mentioned transformations are isometries; they leave the distance between any two points unchanged after the transformation.

a. Reflection
b. Rotation
c. Shear mappings
d. Real matrices

25. The _____ of an m-by-n matrix with real entries is the subspace of R^n generated by the row vectors of the matrix. Its dimension is equal to the rank of the matrix and is at most min(m,n.)

The column space of an m-by-n matrix with real entries is the subspace of R^m generated by the column vectors of the matrix.

a. Restriction of scalars
b. Differential graded algebra
c. Row space
d. Goodman-Nguyen-van Fraassen algebra

26. In linear algebra, a _____ of a matrix A is a nonzero vector v, which has associated with it an eigenvalue λ having algebraic multiplicity k ≥1, satisfying

$$(A - \lambda I)^k \mathbf{v} = 0.$$

Ordinary eigenvectors are obtained for k=1.

Chapter 8. LINEAR PROGRAMMING AND GAME THEORY

Generalized eigenvectors are needed to form a complete basis of a defective matrix, which is a matrix in which there are fewer linearly independent eigenvectors than eigenvalues. The generalized eigenvectors do form a complete basis, as follows from the Jordan form of a matrix.

a. Schmidt decomposition
b. Generalized eigenvector
c. Vectorization
d. Jordan normal form

27. In linear algebra, two n-by-n matrices A and B are called _____ if

$$B = P^{-1}AP$$

for some invertible n-by-n matrix P. _____ matrices represent the same linear transformation under two different bases, with P being the change of basis matrix.

The matrix P is sometimes called a similarity transformation. In the context of matrix groups, similarity is sometimes referred to as conjugacy, with _____ matrices being conjugate.

a. Similar
b. Zero matrix
c. Cartan matrix
d. Skew-symmetric

28. For each eigenvector of a linear transformation, there is a corresponding scalar value called an _____ for that vector, which determines the amount the eigenvector is scaled under the linear transformation. For example, an _____ of +2 means that the eigenvector is doubled in length and points in the same direction. An _____ of +1 means that the eigenvector is unchanged, while an _____ of −1 means that the eigenvector is reversed in sense.

a. Abelian P-root group
b. Eigenvalue
c. ADE classification
d. AKS primality test

29. In mathematics, a _____ is a semigroup in which every element is idempotent The lattice of varieties of bands was described independently by Birjukov, Fennemore and Gerhard. Semilattices, left-zero bands, right-zero bands, rectangular bands and regular bands, specific subclasses of bands which lie near the bottom of this lattice, are of particular interest and are briefly described below.

Chapter 8. LINEAR PROGRAMMING AND GAME THEORY

a. Formal power series
b. Group extension
c. Band
d. Direct product

30. In mathematics, particularly matrix theory, a _____ is a sparse matrix, whose non-zero entries are confined to a diagonal band, comprising the main diagonal and zero or more diagonals on either side.

Formally, an n×n matrix A=($a_{i,j}$) is a _____ if all matrix elements are zero outside a diagonally bordered band whose range is determined by constants k_1 and k_2:

$$a_{i,j} = 0 \quad \text{if} \quad j < i - k_1 \quad \text{or} \quad j > i + k_2; \quad k_1, k_2 \geq 0.$$

The quantities k_1 and k_2 are the left and right half-bandwidth, respectively. The bandwidth of the matrix is $k_1 + k_2 + 1$ (in other words, the smallest number of adjacent diagonals to which the non-zero elements are confined.)

a. Band matrix
b. Binary matrix
c. Modal matrix
d. Skew-symmetric

31. In numerical analysis, the _____ associated with a problem is a measure of that problem's amenability to digital computation, that is, how numerically well-conditioned the problem is. A problem with a low _____ is said to be well-conditioned, while a problem with a high _____ is said to be ill-conditioned.

For example, the _____ associated with the linear equation Ax = b gives a bound on how inaccurate the solution x will be after approximate solution.

a. -module
b. Bernstein polynomial
c. Condition number
d. -equivalence

32. In the case of Gaussian elimination, it is best to choose a pivot element with large absolute value. This improves the numerical stability. In _____, the algorithm considers all entries in the column of the matrix that is currently being considered, picks the entry with largest absolute value, and finally swaps rows such that this entry is the pivot in question.

a. -equivalence
b. Partial pivoting
c. -module
d. 2-bridge knot

33. In mathematics, _____ or factoring is the decomposition of an object ' href='/wiki/Matrix_(mathematics)'>matrix) into a product of other objects, or factors, which when multiplied together give the original. For example, the number 15 factors into primes as 3 × 5, and the polynomial $x^2 - 4$ factors as $(x - 2)(x + 2)$. In all cases, a product of simpler objects is obtained.

a. -equivalence
b. -module
c. 2-bridge knot
d. Factorization

34. In several fields of mathematics the term _____ is used with different but closely related meanings. They all relate to the notion of mapping the elements of a set to other elements of the same set, i.e., exchanging (or 'permuting') elements of a set.

The general concept of _____ can be defined more formally in different contexts:

In combinatorics, a _____ is usually understood to be a sequence containing each element from a finite set once, and only once.

a. Near-field
b. Binary function
c. Rupture field
d. Permutation

ANSWER KEY

Chapter 1
1. b   2. b   3. d   4. d   5. d   6. b   7. d   8. b   9. d   10. b
11. a   12. d   13. d   14. d   15. a   16. d   17. d   18. a   19. d   20. d
21. d   22. d   23. a

Chapter 2
1. a   2. b   3. d   4. d   5. d   6. d   7. d   8. b   9. a   10. d
11. d   12. d   13. c   14. c   15. d   16. d   17. c   18. c   19. a

Chapter 3
1. a   2. d   3. a   4. b   5. d   6. d   7. b   8. c   9. d   10. d
11. d   12. b   13. d   14. d   15. c   16. c   17. c   18. c   19. d   20. d
21. d   22. d   23. c   24. b   25. d   26. d   27. b   28. a   29. a   30. a
31. a   32. d   33. b   34. d   35. d   36. d   37. c   38. d   39. d   40. d
41. d   42. d   43. d   44. b   45. a   46. d   47. a   48. a   49. d

Chapter 4
1. d   2. d   3. d   4. c   5. b   6. c   7. d   8. a   9. a   10. d
11. d   12. a   13. d   14. d   15. c   16. d

Chapter 5
1. d   2. a   3. d   4. d   5. b   6. d   7. a   8. d   9. a   10. d
11. d   12. d   13. a   14. a   15. a   16. d   17. c   18. d   19. a   20. a
21. d   22. d   23. d   24. c   25. a   26. d   27. b   28. a   29. d   30. d
31. c   32. d   33. b   34. c   35. d   36. d   37. d   38. a   39. b   40. a
41. d   42. d   43. d   44. d   45. d   46. d   47. d   48. a   49. b   50. a

Chapter 6
1. d   2. b   3. d   4. d   5. d   6. d   7. a   8. b   9. d   10. b
11. d   12. b   13. d   14. c   15. d   16. c   17. b   18. a   19. a   20. b
21. d

Chapter 7
1. d   2. d   3. d   4. c   5. d   6. d   7. d   8. d   9. d   10. d
11. c   12. b   13. d   14. c   15. a   16. b   17. c   18. a   19. d   20. d
21. d   22. c

Chapter 8
1. d   2. a   3. c   4. b   5. d   6. b   7. a   8. c   9. a   10. c
11. c   12. d   13. d   14. d   15. d   16. b   17. d   18. b   19. d   20. d
21. b   22. c   23. b   24. b   25. c   26. b   27. a   28. b   29. c   30. a
31. c   32. b   33. d   34. d

www.ingramcontent.com/pod-product-compliance
Lightning Source LLC
Chambersburg PA
CBHW081847230426
43669CB00018B/2848